Glyn Rees is a writer, illustrator, book designer and cartoonist with numerous publications to his credit. His work has appeared in *Punch* and many other national newspapers and magazines. He loves all kinds of humorous verse, from Ewart to Spilligan, but is particularly fond of that peculiar, yet enduring, British institution – the limerick!

The Mammoth Book of Limericks

Edited by Glyn Rees

ROBINSON

RUNNING PRESS
PHILADELPHIA · LONDON

Constable & Robinson Ltd
3 The Lanchesters
162 Fulham Palace Road
London W6 9ER
www.constablerobinson.com

First published in the UK by Robinson,
an imprint of Constable & Robinson, 2008

A copy of the British Library Cataloguing in Publication
Data is available from the British Library

UK ISBN 978-1-84529-681-0

1 3 5 7 9 10 8 6 4 2

First published in the United States in 2008 by Running Press Book Publishers
All rights reserved under the Pan-American and International Copyright Conventions

9   8   7   6   5   4   3   2   1
Digit on the right indicates the number of this printing

US Library of Congress number: 2008931719
US ISBN 978-0-7624-3395-7

Running Press Book Publishers
2300 Chestnut Street
Philadelphia, PA 19103-4371
www.runningpress.com

Visit us on the web!

www.runningpress.com

Printed and bound in the EU

Contents

Introduction

Most people believe that a gentleman called Edward Lear, an artist
and writer who was to become Drawing Master to Queen
Victoria, invented the modern limerick. He did not, though he
unquestionably helped to popularize the form in his *Book of
Nonsense*, published initially in 1846, and reprinted in 1863.
Limericks, or something very like them, had been around long
before that.

The origins of the limerick are a matter of speculation. Classical
scholars will argue that the first examples were composed around
400 BC by the Ancient Greeks. Their greatest comic poet,
Aristophanes, may certainly have tried his hand at this curious but
interesting verse form, which has inexplicably endured as the most
popular in the English language.

There are rhymes closely resembling the limerick in the British
Museum; this is from the Harleian Manuscript, dating from the
fourteenth century:

> The lion is wondirliche strong,
> & ful of wiles of wo;
>   & wether he pleye
>   other take his preye
> he can not do bot slo. (slay)

After this, there is no evidence of the limerick for almost two
hundred years, until its reappearance in the late sixteenth century
in the songs of the mad "bedlams" – half-naked beggars,

wandering the streets of England and Ireland. The most familiar of their songs, "Mad Tom" or "Tom o' Bedlam", was first noted in a manuscript music book around 1615, though it was probably decades old by then. Here is a sample verse:

> From the hagg & hungry Goblin,
> That into rags would rend yee,
> > & the spirit that stand's
> > by the naked man,
> in the books of moones defend yee…

Shakespeare's work contains verses that are identifiable as limericks. In *Hamlet* for instance, Ophelia, distraught, with her hair in disarray, sings to the accompaniment of her lute:

> His beard was as white as snow,
> All flaxen was his poll,
> > He is gone, he is gone,
> > And we cast away moan,
> God ha' mercy on his soul!

In *Othello*, Iago calls for wine and bursts into song:

> And let me the canakin clink, clink;
> And let me the canakin clink;
> > A soldier's a man;
> > Oh, man's life's but a span;
> Why, then, let a soldier drink.

And this is Stephano's song from *The Tempest*, about a ship's crew who "Loved Moll, Meg and Marian, But none of us cared for Kate":

> For she had a tongue with a tang,
> Would cry to a sailor: 'Go hang':
>   She loved not the savour of tar nor of pitch,
>   Yet a tailor might scratch her where'er she did itch –
> Then to sea, boys, and let her go hang.

Although the third and fourth lines are longer, instead of shorter, than the other three, this is still reminiscent of the limerick form.

Robert Herrick, a contemporary of Shakespeare's, also employed the limerick form. Here are a couple of stanzas from his 1648 love poem *The Night-piece: to Julia*:

> Her Eyes the Glow-worms lend thee,
> The Shooting Starres attend thee;
>   And the Elves also
>   Whose little eyes glow,
> Like the sparks of fire, befriend thee.

> Then Julia let me wooe thee,
> Thus, thus to come unto me;
>   And when I shall meet
>   Thy silv'ry feet,
> My soule Ile poure into thee.

Here is an even clearer example, from the poem *Upon Jone and Jane*:

> Jane is a Girle that's prittie;
> Jane is a wench that's wittie;
>   Yet, who wo'd think
>   Her breath do's stink,
> As so it doth? that's pittie.

And, during the latter part of the eighteenth century, the Irish poet Thomas Moore wrote his love poem *The Young May Moon*, of which this is the opening verse:

> The Young May moon is beaming, love,
> The glow-worm's lamp is gleaming, love;
>   How sweet to rove
>   Through Morne's grove
> When the drowsy world is dreaming, love.
> Then awake! – the heavens look bright, my dear,
> 'Tis never too late for delight, my dear,
>   And the best of all ways
>   To lengthen our days
> Is to steal a few hours from the night, my dear!

Over twenty years before Lear's work, two other books had appeared: *The History of Sixteen Wonderful Old Women, illustrated with as many engravings: exhibiting their Eccentricities and Amusements* is widely accepted as the first published collection of limericks, although the term "limerick" was not in use at that time. *Anecdotes and Adventures of Fifteen Gentlemen* followed a couple of years later. Edward Lear will almost certainly have seen these books. At least two of his rhymes, and their illustrations, appear to be based on characters in the earlier publications. The verses in those books were of a fairly innocuous nature, as indeed were Lear's own, though they were soon being parodied by others:

> There was a Young Lady from Norway
> Who casually sat in a doorway;
> When the door squeezed her flat,
> She exclaimed: "What of that?"
> This courageous Young Lady of Norway.

very quickly became:

> There was a Young Lady from Norway
> Who hung by her toes in a doorway;
> She said to her beau:
> "Just look at me, Joe,
> I think I've discovered one more way!"

probably at the hands of the mischievous Algernon Charles Swinburne (1837–1909), a well-known poet and contemporary of Alfred Lord Tennyson, himself reputed to have written a handful of bawdy limericks.

This may have been the beginning of the indecent (or bawdy) limerick, although it is more likely that the clean and indecent varieties had existed side by side for some time. Perhaps, in the same way that Lear popularized the one kind, Swinburne and his friends popularized the other. Both can be equally entertaining and are perfectly acceptable today, provided that they are well-constructed, clever and, most importantly of all – funny!

A "limerick limerick" neatly sums up this hypothesis:

It needn't have ribaldry's taint,
Or strive to make everyone faint;
   There's a type that's demure
   And perfectly pure,
Though it helps quite a lot if it ain't!

Limericks, or verses with a strong family likeness, have always been evident in our traditional nursery rhymes (think of Hickory, Dickory Dock and Goosey, Goosey Gander), lullabies, chants, counting games, and even Christmas carols, as these two sample verses illustrate:

We three Kings of Orient are;
Bearing gifts we traverse afar,
   Field and fountain,
   Moor and mountain,
Following yonder star.

Frankincense to offer have I,
Incense owns a Deity nigh,
   Prayer and praising,
   All men raising,
Worship Him, God most high.

This is a particularly amusing children's street chant from the mid-1920s:

Mickey Mouse was in his house
Taking off his trousers;
   Then his mum
   Smacked his bum,
And chased him round the houses.

SO, WHY IS A LIMERICK CALLED A LIMERICK?

Evidence of the use of the limerick form as a chorus in drinking-songs was seen in England around 1610, antedating by almost a century the presumed use of such choruses in Ireland. This is from the round-song *Now That the Spring Hath Filled our Veins* by one William Browne:

> Shear sheep that have them, cry we still,
> But see that no man 'scape
>   To drink of the sherry
>   That makes us so merry,
> And plump as the lusty grape.

However, more widespread opinion appears to link the limerick verse form with the Irish town of that name. According to the *Oxford English Dictionary*, the word is "said to be from a custom at convivial parties, according to which each member sang an extemporized 'nonsense verse', which was followed by a chorus containing the words 'Will you come up to Limerick?'. Other reference books carry a similar definition.

It has been suggested that the name "limerick" is directly connected with the 1691 Treaty of Limerick which brought peace between England and Ireland, and released many thousands of trained Irish soldiers to fight as mercenaries as part of "The Irish Brigade" in France. Its cavalry, interestingly, was commanded by the Earl of Limerick. It is quite likely that members of the Brigade encountered a few old French verses in the limerick form, including this version of Hickory, Dickory Dock:

Digerie, Digerie, doge,
La souris ascend l'horloge,
  L'horloge frappe,
  La souris s'echappe,
Digerie, Digerie, doge.

The form of rhyme which had long been popular in France evidently became equally popular with her Irish Allies. And, when it became more widespread in Britain, and needed a general title, the one already in use in Ireland was adopted.

Cyril Bibby, a biologist and educator and one of the first sexologists, in his book *The Art of the Limerick*, rather mischievously puts forward the theory that the limerick might have been named after some historical or even fictional figure:

"Since the fourth Earl of Sandwich, who found that the most convenient form of sustenance during his long sessions at the gaming tables was cold beef between slices of toasted bread, inspired that handy word 'sandwich'; since Wellington boots were so named after the great Duke of Wellington; since the mackintosh raincoat, so admirably suited to the unpredictable rains of his native hills, was named after Charles Mackintosh; since the 'raglan' style of overcoat-shouldering recalls Lord Fitzroy Somerset, first Baron Raglan; and since women's bloomers immortalized the American suffragist Mrs Amelia Bloomer; why should not limericks be called after somebody of that name? 'Limerick' as a surname, or a forename, sounds no more unlikely than 'clerihew', which became the name of a type of verse invented by Edmund Clerihew Bentley."

Another suggestion for the origin of the word, is that it is a combination of the two words "learic" and "limmer". Learic (no longer in use) was a term newly invented in 1898 for a single stanza poem like those that appeared in Lear's *Book of Nonsense* – a juxtaposition of "lyric" and "lear". Limmer was a word that appeared in *The English Dialect Dictionary* meaning "a scoundrel, rascal, rogue or prostitute, strumpet, a loose, immoral woman or girl". What better term for the often dubious or unsavoury characters who would have been popping up, especially in the bawdier limerick offerings of the time!

AND WHAT ACTUALLY *IS* A LIMERICK?

Part of the difficulty in determining how far back the limerick may be traced in English Literature, lies in the lack of any precise definition of the form. What, for instance, is one to make of Thomas Moore's *The Young May Moon (see page 10)*? Clearly the content has more sophistication than one normally associates with limericks, but from the point of view of rhyming and scansion it consists of perfect limerick quintains, modified only by the addition of "love" and "my dear" at the ends of the longer lines.

For the uninitiated, and in very simple terms, a limerick consists of five lines rhyming *aabba*. There are usually nine "beats" in lines one, two and five; six "beats" in lines three and four; the third, sixth and ninth "beats'in lines one, two and five being accented; ditty-*dum*, ditty-*dum*, ditty-*dum*. Scholars call this anapaestic foot. In truth, many different types of metrical feet have been used successfully in limericks. After all, such verses exist primarily to be heard rather than looked at! Thomas Campion (1575–1620) commented: "The ear is a rational sense, and a chief judge of proportion". Swinburne, as you might expect, later put it more directly: "A dunce like myself measures verse by ear, and not by finger!"

But there is more to any form of verse than its mere rhyming and metre. Just as the sonnet has always seemed especially suited to the expression of tender passion, so there is something about the limerick peculiarly appropriate to nonsense, wit and bawdiness. A writer, in *The Times Literary Supplement*, once, rather heavy-handedly, described the limerick as being "essentially liturgical, corresponding to the underlying ritual of Greek tragedy, with the *parados* (initial entry) of the first line, the *peripeteia* (change of situation) of the second, the *stichomythia* (development from earlier statements) of the two shorter lines, and the *epiphaneia* (final showing) in the last.

The author Paul Jennings has remarked that limericks have "a kind of inevitability, a quality of something found just lying there, occurring naturally, like the first diamonds". Morris Bishop, American scholar, historian, biographer, humorist, and a brilliant limerick writer himself, said that their "structure should rise from the commonplace reality of line one to logical madness in line five". Arthur Wimperis, who wrote so many great British musical comedies, said: "The only limericks in my experience of any literary merit are distinctly Rabelaisian. Beside these, the more polite and printable examples fade away into the dim haze of mediocrity". Don Marquis, another humorist from across the Atlantic, divided limericks into three distinct types: "Limericks to be told when ladies are present; limericks to be told when ladies are absent, but clergymen are present – and LIMERICKS!" And Cyril Bibby suggested that the limerick is to poetry in general what the caricature is to graphic art.

The best limericks tend to be conversational, and flow fluidly. Compactness is an essential ingredient. Someone else insisted, rather grandly, that there were few poetical forms that could boast the limerick's perfection, it having "progression, development, variety, speed, climax and high mnemonic value". Mnemonic? Of, or designed to aid the memory.

As to the content of limericks: "Themes are so diverse, that it does not seem to matter what they are – lively incidents and keenly-drawn characters – wild extravagances – invitations to irresponsibility – illustrations of violence". So wrote Peter and Iona Opie, well-known folklorists and anthologists, about nursery rhymes, and the same may be said of limericks.

Louis Untermeyer, a New Yorker who not only wrote himself, but was also a respected editor and anthologist, has said: "After Lear, the limerick grew fantastically. It embraced every topic, territory and temperament; nothing was too sacred or too obscene for those five small lines. The limerick absorbed solemnities and absurdities, traditional legends and off-colour jokes, devout reflections and downright indecencies, without a quiver of the loss of a syllable".

Another writer, H. I. Brock summed it all up: "Nothing human is excluded from its range. In politics, divinity, philosophy, philology, sociology, zoology; in botany, Latinity, relativity, revelry and ribaldry; it is equally at home. Geography is its happy hunting ground. Matters vegetable, animal and mineral are grist to its mill. Love, sacred and profane, is fair game. Bishops and tabby cats are equal targets. And the follies, foibles, fortunes, failures and fallacies to which our mortal flesh is heir, from the cradle to the grave, are the stuff to which its antics give the *coup de pied*."

The continuing popularity of the limerick has been partly due to its suitability as a basis for competitions, either in newspapers and magazines (and even television programmes), or linked to consumer products. At the beginning of the twentieth century, limerick writing became particularly popular when several publications, such as *Punch*, *The Sunday Times* and the *Yorkshire Post* – ran regular *weekly* competitions. Entrants were required variously to supply last lines, the first four lines to a given last line or complete verses. Prizes ranged from £3 a week for life (a lot of money in 1908) to an all-expenses paid, round-trip for two to the Irish town of Limerick with a fistful of spending money thrown in!

The popularity of the limerick led naturally to the publication of numerous books. In 1925, journalist Langford Reed compiled *The Complete Limerick Book* in Britain, whilst at virtually the same time, across the Atlantic, the author Carolyn Wells was collecting together her *Book of American Limericks*. Both books contained what might be called "clean" examples of the verse form. The first modern book of indecent, or bawdy (call them what you will) limericks, appropriately titled *The Limerick*, was published in 1974 by Gershon Legman, and contained over 1,700 verses!

Limerick books have appeared regularly ever since, as the Bibliography at the back of this book testifies. Though many may have earned money by publishing limericks, it is doubtful whether anyone has ever earned a living from them. Most limerick writing has been done for enjoyment – of the writer and the reader. It has largely, but certainly not exclusively, been the literary pursuit of the amateur. Any list of today's foremost limerick writers, for adults or children, has to include Gerard Benson, Paul Cookson, Gavin Ewart, Cyril Fletcher, Edward Gorey, Reg Lynes, Charlotte McBee, Colin McNaughton, Spike Milligan, Ogden Nash, Michael Palin, Frank Richards, Ron Rubin, Nick Toczek, and Colin West.

It has been suggested that a straightforward collection of limericks would be boring. The restricted pattern of the metre would lend itself to monotony. Yet one cannot deny the astonishing variety of the material written in this simple verse form. There is sophisticated wit, and bawdy humour, satire and barbed social comment, nonsense and fantasy, wry irony and even quite serious limericks. The spectrum is too broad for there to be any danger of boredom. Besides which, surely a limerick anthology is a book to be browsed, or dipped into from time to time, rather than something that readers would choose to read straight through from cover to cover.

In the Foreword to his *Book of Limericks*, published in Paris in 1955, Count Palmiro Vicarion (widely believed to be the pseudonym of poet Christopher Logue) insisted:

> "The limerick is precious, an exquisite thing; like a good burgundy, it should not be taken indifferently, too often, or in unduly large quantities. Only a fool, I repeat, a fool would gulp down a glass of Chambertin, or read this book in a sitting…"

Glyn Rees

LIMERICK COMPETITIONS

The innocuous limerick competitions run regularly by *Punch*
magazine in the 1860s, came to an abrupt halt with the
anonymous submission of a disconcerting number of bawdy and
sacrilegious examples. These "indecent" verses, which immediately
began to circulate orally, were reputed to be the work of, amongst
others, the poet Swinburne, a gentleman already with an
established reputation for secret poetry and erotic prose.

Still, limericks have continued to be popular, particularly during
the early 1900s, as the basis of competitions organized by other
newspapers and periodicals, or by manufacturers promoting their
products. Typically, the first four lines of a limerick would be
provided, with the public invited to think of a suitable tag line.
Such competitions very quickly assumed "craze" proportions,
despite competitors often having to part with an entry fee of as
much as sixpence! In a speech he made before the House of
Commons on 17 July 1908, a Mr Buxton said: "During the last six
months of 1907, the public, in the normal run of things, would
have bought between 700,000 and 800,000 sixpenny postal
orders. They actually purchased no less than 1,400,000 – fourteen
times as much!"

The prize offered by Traylee Cigarettes, for providing the last line
to their incomplete limerick, was £3 a week for life. This was the
challenge:

That the Traylee's the best cigarette,
Is a "tip" that we cannot forget;
    And in buying I'll mention
    There's a three pound a week pension –

And this was the winning line, sent in by a Mr R. Rhodes, of Cardiff:

Two good "lines" – one you give, one you get.

Another competition, run by the American magazine *Business Week*, departed from the standard format by requesting that entrants write the first four lines of a limerick ending with: "It isn't how many... it's who!" There was a second prize of $500, a third prize of $250 and twelve portable typewriters for runners-up. The first prize was a round-trip for two to Limerick in southern Ireland, all expenses paid. The winners stayed at the historic Dromoland Castle, toured the coast of County Clare, played golf at the best championship courses, kissed the Blarney Stone, lunched with the Mayor of Limerick, and met the Lord mayor of Dublin during a visit to the Abbey Theatre – altogether a two week trip, with $500 spending money thrown in! The 1,443 entrants submitted over 4,000 limericks, and the first prize was won by Alexander Ross, from New York City, who wrote:

If it's management men you pursue,
Don't hunt every beast in the Zoo;
    Just look for the signs
    That say: "Tigers and lions" –
It isn't how many... it's who!

When the *Sunday Mirror* announced a competition for verses that were "funny, publishable, and above all ORIGINAL", with cash prizes for every limerick published, and £50 for the best, 7,000 hopeful entries were received. The paper insisted that "everybody has a favourite – from drawing-room decorous to saloon bar saucy – all of them with a special rhyming rhythm, playing on words and pronunciation, and with a jokey pay-off". Here are a couple of the successful verses:

> There was a young lady from Cheam
> Who tried out a breast-growing cream;
>> She woke in the night
>> With a terrible fright –
> Another had grown in between!

and

> A surgeon of some imprecision,
> Decided on self-circumcision;
>> A slip of the knife –
>> "Oh, dear," said his wife,
> "Our sex-life will need some revision."

The *Daily Mail*, which still regularly publishes readers' limericks, offered bottles of champagne as prizes in one of its limerick competitions, which produced these winning entries:

> A nasty old vampire named Dracula
> Had habits considered spectacula;
>> He drank by the keg,
>> But 'twas pure rhesus neg –
> Red Barrel, to use the vernacular!

When they catch a chinchilla in Chile,
They cut off its beard, willy-nilly,
   With a small razor blade,
   Just to say that they've made
A Chilean chinchilla's chin chilly.

The limerick is clearly very much alive and well, particularly orally, popping up regularly in both television and radio programmes. It is still used from time to time by publications such as the *New Statesman,* the *Spectator,* and the *Oldie,* as a convenient device to elicit witty and clever competition submissions from its subscribers.

LIMERICKS BY "CELEBRITIES"

Limericks are not exclusively written by our old friend, the ubiquitous Anonymous. There are numerous examples by many eminent poets, novelists and humorists.

Alfred, Lord Tennyson (1809–1892), a contemporary of Swinburne, is supposed to have written several outstanding erotic limericks (perhaps as light relief from composing the sickly stanzas of his *Idylls of the King*), all of which were destroyed when he died, presumably to protect his fine reputation.

And Queen Elizabeth I is believed to have *almost* composed this example, which may be found in *The Oxford Book of English Verse*:

> The daughter of debate
> Who discord aye doth sow,
>   Hath reaped no gain
>   Where former reign
> Hath taught still peace to grow.

George Bernard Shaw was a great lover of limericks, though he was dismayed that so many of his favourites were, in his time, considered unfit for publication. He observed: "They must be passed on through oral tradition, but it may be that, in the course of time, sufficient limericks which shall be decent as well as witty or ingenious may accumulate". Shaw may have written The Old Man from St Bees (a parody of Edward Lear), although it is more widely attributed to the librettist W. S. Gilbert of Gilbert and Sullivan.

Gilbert, despite an impatience with Lear, was fond of the limerick form, and used it in much of his work. This is from *The Sorcerer*:

> Oh, my name is John Wellington Wells,
> I'm a dealer in magic and spells,
>   Of blessings and curses,
>   And ever-filled purses,
> In prophecies, witches and knells.

Rudyard Kipling refers to the limerick in his story *Stalky*: "Make up a good limerick, and let the fags sing it". He himself wrote:

> There once was a boy of Quebec
> Who was buried in snow to his neck;
>   When asked: "Are you frizz?"
>   He replied: "Yes, I is –
> But we don't call this cold in Quebec!"

Bertrand Russell, philosopher, mathematician and winner of the Nobel Prize for Literature, is supposedly the author of:

> There was a young girl of Shanghai
> Who was so exceedingly shy,
>   That, undressing at night,
>   She turned out the light,
> For fear of the All-Seeing Eye.

John Galsworthy, another recipient of the Nobel Prize for Literature, is credited with:

To an artist a husband named Bicket
Said: "Turn your backside, and I'll kick it.
    You have painted my wife
    In the nude to the life;
Do you think for the moment that's cricket?"

The Reverend Patrick Brontë, father of the extraordinary trio of
novelist sisters wrote poetry. *The Cottage Maid*, composed in
1811, contains 24 stanzas all written so nearly in limerick form,
bar the almost perversely non-rhyming final lines. Here is a typical
verse:

Aloft on the brow of a mountain,
And hard by a clear running fountain,
    In neat little cot,
    Content with her lot,
Retired, there lives a sweet maiden.

Robert Louis Stevenson is known to have written at least one
limerick, which possibly helped to take the "place-name" variety out
of the British Isles and extend its range to other parts of the world:

There was an old man of the Cape
Who made himself garments of crepe;
    When asked: "Do they tear?"
    He replied: "Here and there,
But they're perfectly splendid for shape!"

The humorist, Gelert Burgess, who added to the English language
such words as "blurb" and "bromide", and will always be
remembered as the man who wrote "I never saw a purple cow",
also gave us many limericks, including these two:

I wish that my room had a floor;
I don't care so much for a door;
    But this walking around
    Without touching the ground
Is getting to be quite a bore.

I'd rather have fingers than toes;
I'd rather have ears than a nose;
    And as for my hair,
    I'm glad that it's there –
I'll be awfully sad when it goes.

Statesmen, as well as writers, ambassadors, vice-presidents and at least one President of the United States – have had fun with what is sometimes referred to as "terse form". Joseph Kennedy, father of the late President John F. Kennedy, wrote, shortly after the Treaty of Versailles ended World War 1:

Says the Frenchman: "You'll pay us for sure."
Says the German: "We can't for we're poor."
    So Fritz with a whine
    Sings his "Watch on the Rhine",
But the Poilu sings "Watch on the Ruhr".

Vice-President Alben Barkley composed:

In New Orleans dwelt a young Creole
Who, when asked if her hair was all reole,
    Replied, with a shrug:
    "Just give it a tug,
And decide by the way that I squeole."

And of course Clement Attlee, who was British Prime Minister between 1945 and 1951, offered a famous rebuff to his detractors in limerick form:

Few thought he was even a starter,
There were many who thought themselves smarter;
   But he ended PM,
   CH and OM,
An Earl and a Knight of the Garter.

LIMERICKS FROM ELSEWHERE

Although the occasional foreign phrases – usually French or Latin – do crop up within its lines, the limerick, according to Louis Untermeyer, may be considered "as English as cricket, Big Ben, or afternoon tea and crumpets". The longer one studies limericks, the more one is struck by their overwhelmingly strong affiliation with English.

A Washington professor agreed that the limerick is, without doubt, Anglo-American – perhaps, as had been observed long ago, the *only* original verse form of the English language.

It has been suggested that limericks have flourished as a manifestation of some peculiarly English streak of nonsensicality. Certain features of the language have also played an important part: its great economy allows the compression of complete statements into very short lines; its characteristically strong stressing is suited to the oral repetition of humorous or satirical verse; its marvellously rich and varied vocabulary facilitates the task of any versifier struggling for a third-rhyme ending to the limerick's fifth and final line.

There are a few scattered specimens, such as *Digerie, Digerie, Doge* in native French literature, but nothing approaching the vast wealth to be found in the English language.

Here are a few verses by George du Maurier, the British author and cartoonist born in Paris in 1834, and grandfather of novelist Daphne du Maurier:

Un Marin naufrage (de Doncastre)
Pour priere, au milieu du desastre,
   Repetait à genoux
   Ces mots simples et doux –
"Scintillez, scintillez, petit astre!"

A Cologne est un maître d'hotel
Hors du centre du ventre duquel
   Se projette une sorte
   De tiroir qui supporte
La moutarde, et le poivre, et le sel.

Il existe une Espinstere à Tours,
Un peu vite, et qui porte toujours
   Un ulsteur peau-de-phoque,
   Un chapeau bilicoque,
Et des nicrebocqueurs en velours.

There is very little in German, apart from a handful of what
appear to be awkward translations from English originals:

Ein dicklicher mann in Peru
Der traumte mal von einer kuh;
   Und alse r erwacht
   Da ha ter gelacht :
Seine frau stand am bett und macht "Muh!"

A plumpish chap in Peru
Was dreaming about a cow;
   When he awoke,
   He couldn't help laughing –
His wife was standing at the bedside saying "Moo!"

The Welsh word for "limerick" is something very similar – *limrig*.
Here is an example:

Yr oedd ffermwr yn byw draw yn llyn
A chornwydydd yn blatsh ar ei din:
    Aeth draw i Bwllheli
    I gael bocsed o eli,
A wir, erbyn hyn does dim un.

A farmer who lived near a lake
Had hundreds of spots, boils, sores, etc. on his bum;
    So he went to Pwllheli
    To purchase some ointment,
And it worked – now he doesn't have one!

LIMERICK ILLUSTRATIONS

Being an accomplished writer *and* artist, who eventually became
Drawing Master to Queen Victoria, it is no surprise that the
limericks in Edward Lear's *Book of Nonsense* were accompanied
by his own pen and ink illustrations.

Lear did not actually *invent* the limerick, he merely helped
popularize it. But he can be credited with establishing the
tradition of the illustrated limerick, although several of his
drawings bear a strong resemblance to drawings from the very
first book of limericks – *The History of Sixteen Wonderful Old
Women, illustrated with as many engravings, exhibiting their
Eccentricities and Amusements* – which was published
over twenty years earlier. This is Lear's Old Person of Harrow and
its illustration, together with the original drawing from the earlier
book:

There was an Old Person of Harrow
Who bought a mahogany barrow;
   For he said to his wife:
   "You're the joy of my life!
And I'll wheel you all day in this barrow!"

Since Lear's book, the majority of limerick collections have been wholly or partly illustrated. Such books have always attracted the top-class professional cartoonists of their time. The Australian, H. M. Bateman, one of *Punch* magazine's most famous contributors, provided the drawings for Langford Reed's *The Complete Limerick Book*, a classic compilation which was published in 1925:

> There was a young lady of Riga,
> Who went for a ride on a tiger;
>   They returned from the ride
>   With the lady inside,
> And a smile on the face of the tiger.

At the same time, across the Atlantic in America, *The Book of American Limericks*, collected by Carolyn Wells, was accompanied with illustrations by an uncredited artist:

> There was a discreet Brigadier,
> Very fond of Four Thousand a year;
>   Who, when he heard the guns rattle,
>   Fiercely cried: "Ha! The battle!"
> Then complacently slid to the rear.

The more amateur, do-it-yourself approach has also produced entertaining results: John Sephton, always more of a writer than an artist, took the plunge and illustrated his collection of *Lancashire Limericks* with his own quirky line drawings:

A serious young fellow from Colne
Used to go on long-bike rides alone;
   Till a lass said: "Abandon
   Your bike for a tandem!"
Now he grins like a dog with a bone.

And the consistently funny Ron Rubin's collection, *A Child's Garden of Limericks*, was adorned with delightful drawings by his eight-year-old granddaughter Mabyn Aita:

We've got two pet dogs, Scamp and Scruff,
Scruff's playful, but Scamp is quite rough;
    Each day I take Scamp
    And we go for a tramp,
But the tramp says he's had quite enough.

Contemporary cartoonists and illustrators have been, and are continually being asked to visualize limericks both old and new. Tony Ross, a marvellous children's book illustrator, has supplied the drawings for several books. So too have John Jensen, another *Punch* cartoonist, and Peter Firmin, the co-creator (with Oliver Postgate) of *The Clangers* TV series for children. Quentin Blake, famous amongst other things for his long and fruitful collaboration with author Roald Dahl, has illustrated a book of green limericks. This collection has been illustrated by Tim Archbold, an emerging talent in the field of children's picture books. And Noel Ford, another *Punch* legend, who has also drawn for the *New Yorker*, has produced a book of cleverly and aptly named *Limeroons*, written and illustrated by himself, which clearly embraces and continues the Lear tradition:

As my husky-team started to sneeze,
And tremble and shake at the knees,
   I knew that I oughta
   Put into their water
A little drop more antifreeze.

LIMERICK FACTFILE

Edward Lear died on 26 January 1888, at St Remo on the Italian Riviera. Only a couple of years later, the word "limerick" made its first appearance in the *Oxford English Dictionary*, defined as "an indecent nonsense verse".

The earliest collection of erotic limericks is believed to have been the twelve-page *New Book of Nonsense* published in London in 1868.

The Limerick (edited by the American, Gershon Legman), the closest thing to a definitive modern collection of bawdy limericks that has ever appeared, was published in Paris in 1974. More than 500 pages contain almost 1,800 examples. Chapter headings in the book include: Organs, Strange Intercourse, Oral Irregularities, Abuses of the Clergy, Excrement, Sex Substitutes and Assorted Eccentricities!

Edward Gorey, the American writer and illustrator, and master of macabre and gothic limericks, used a number of different pseudonyms for his work, several of which are weird and wonderful anagrams of his own name, such as Ogdred Weary, E. G. Deadworry, Raddory Gewe. Another of his pen-names is Eduard Blutig – "blutig" being the German word for "bloody" which is, of course, a synonym for "gory".

"Bawd" is an old word for a brothel-keeper. It comes from a French word "baude", meaning merry or lively. Bawdy stories therefore, are the sort that contain lighthearted reference to sexual activities, such as might be associated with brothels. Hence: bawdy limericks!

When his ninth, and final book appears in the bookshops in 2008, Birmingham journalist John Slim, who lives appropriately in Lickey End, Worcestershire, will have published more (mostly bawdy) limericks than anyone else in the world – almost 9,000 ! He has approached *The Guinness Book of Records*, but so far they show no inclination to include his extraordinary achievement within their pages. Nevertheless, John is determined to keep trying until he is successful.

R. V. Knox, a renowned writer and collector of limericks, probably started the fashion for writing such verses in different forms many years ago when he placed this "advertisement" in the Classified columns of *The Times* newspaper:

An Anglican curate in want of a second-hand, portable font would exchange for the same a portrait (in frame) of the Bishop-elect of Vermont.

In French, a limerick is a "poème humoristique en cinq lignes", and in German, the not dissimilar "5-zeiliger nonsensvers". The Spanish say: "copla humoristica, especie de aleluya". Aleluya means a cheap verse and also is a colloquialism for "hooray"!

THE WORLD'S WORST LIMERICK!

Everyone has a favourite limerick.
But are there any really *bad* limericks? Of course there are.

Sir William Schwenck Gilbert (1836–1911), better known as
W. S. Gilbert, collaborator with the great composer of light-
opera Sir Arthur Sullivan (1842–1900), and perhaps the cleverest
rhymer of his time, might have produced a chronically bad
example when he wrote:

> There was an old man of St Bees
> Who was stung in the arm by a Wasp;
> > When asked: "Does it hurt?"
> > He replied: "No, it doesn't;
> I'm so glad it wasn't a Hornet."

but this was simply his response to one of Edward Lear's limericks,
with which the irascible Gilbert professed to have little patience:

> There was an old man in a tree
> Who was horribly bored by a bee;
> > When they said: "Does it buzz?"
> > He replied: "Yes, it does!
> It's a regular brute of a bee."

And this apparently hopeless attempt might have been considered
a suitable candidate for the World's Worst, if you did not know
that it has been deliberately written as a silly, nonsensical verse,
again, possibly, in parody of Lear:

There was an old man with a duck
Who was an old man with a duck;
   The duck with the man
   Said: "Look, I'm in luck!
I'm the duck with the man with the duck!"

There certainly have been (and probably will be) many many, let's call them, *less-than-brilliant* examples of limericks, but this poor specimen is widely accepted to be the absolute World's Worst. It is quoted here exactly as it was received some years ago in a competition organized by the popular *Titbits* magazine:

I met a smart damsel at Copenhagen,
With her pretty face I was very much taken;
   "What!" she said, "Turned-up trousers – a London man!
   Fall in love with a crank I never can."
She turned up her nose and away she ran.

Early Limericks

Here's brandy! Come fill up your tumbler,
Or ale if your liking be humbler,
   And while you've a shilling,
   Keep filling and swilling –
A fig for the growls of the grumbler!
JOHN O'TUOMY (1706–77)

I like when I'm quite at my leisure
Mirth, music and all sorts of pleasure;
   When Margery's bringing
   The glass, I like singing
With bards, if they drink within measure.
JOHN O'TUOHY

The time I've lost in wooing,
In watching and pursuing
The light that lies
In women's eyes
Has been my heart's undoing.

Though wisdom oft has sought me,
I scorned the lore she brought me;
   My only books
   Were women's looks,
And folly's all they've taught me.
THOMAS MOORE (1779–1852)

There was an old woman of Leeds
Who spent all her life in good deeds;
  She worked for the poor
  Till her fingers were sore,
This pious old woman of Leeds.
THE HISTORY OF SIXTEEN WONDERFUL OLD WOMEN (1820)

There was an old woman of Gloster
Whose parrot two guineas it cost her;
  But his tongue never ceasing,
  Was vastly displeasing
To that talkative woman of Gloster.
THE HISTORY OF SIXTEEN WONDERFUL OLD WOMEN (1820)

There was an old miser of Reading,
Had a house, with a yard, with a shed in;
  'Twas meant for a cow,
  But so small that I vow
The poor creature could scarce get its head in.
ANECDOTES AND ADVENTURES OF FIFTEEN GENTLEMEN (1822)

There was a sick man of Tobago,
Lived long on rice-gruel and sago;
  But at last, to his bliss,
  The physician said this:
"To a roast leg of mutton you may go."
ANECDOTES AND ADVENTURES OF FIFTEEN GENTLEMEN (1822)

There was an Old Man in a boat,
Who said: "I'm afloat! I'm afloat!"
When they said: "No, you ain't!"
He was ready to faint,
That unhappy Old Man in a boat.

There was an Old Lady of Chertsey
Who made a remarkable curtsey;
    She twirled round and round,
    Till she sunk underground,
Which distressed all the people of Chertsey.

There was an Old Person of Florence,
Who held mutton chops in abhorrence;
    He purchased a Bustard,
    And fried him in Mustard,
Which choked that Old Person of Florence.

There was an Old Man of the Coast,
Who placidly sat on a post;
    But when it was cold,
    He relinquished his hold,
And called for some hot buttered toast.

                There was an Old Lady whose folly
                    Induced her to sit in a holly;
                    Whereupon, by a thorn
                      Her dress being torn,
                    She quickly became melancholy.

There was an Old Man with a Beard,
Who said: "It is just as I feared! –
    Two Owls and a Hen,
    Four Larks and a Wren,
Have all built their nests in my Beard!"

        There was an Old Person of Skye,
        Who waltz'd with a bluebottle fly;
          They buzz'd a sweet tune
          To the light of the moon,
        And entranced all the people of Skye.

There was an Old Person of Gretna
Who rushed down the crater of Etna;
    When they said: "Is it hot?"
    She replied: "No, it's not!"
That mendacious Old Person of Gretna.

There was a Young Person whose history
Was always considered a mystery;
    She sate in a ditch,
    Although no one knew which,
And composed a small treatise on history.

There was an Old Person of Brigg,
Who purchased no end of a Wig;
 So that only his nose
 And the end of his toes
Could be seen when he walked about Brigg.

There was an Old Man who said: "How
Shall I flee from that horrible cow?
 I will sit on this stile,
 And continue to smile,
Which may soften the heart of that cow."

There was an Old Person of Dean,
Who dined on one pea and one bean;
For he said: "More than that
Would make me too fat,"
That cautious Old Person of Dean.

There was an Old Person of Wilts
Who constantly walked upon stilts;
 He wreathed them with lilies
 And daffy-down-dillies,
That elegant Person of Wilts.

There was an Old Man in a Tree,
Whose whiskers were lovely to see;
But the birds of the air
Pluck'd them perfectly bare,
To make themselves nests in that Tree.

There was an Old Person of Putney
Whose food was roast spiders and chutney,
    Which he took with his tea,
    Within sight of the sea,
That romantic Old Person of Putney.

There was an Old Man of Spithead
Who opened the window and said:
    "Fil-jomble, fil-jumble,
    Fil-rumble-come-tumble!"
That doubtful Old Man of Spithead.

There was an old person of Filey,
Of whom his acquaintance spoke highly;
    He danced perfectly well
    To the sound of a bell,
And delighted the people of Filey.

There was an old lady of Winchelsea,
Who said: "If you needle or pin shall see
On the floor of my room,
Sweep it up with the broom!"
That exhaustive old lady of Winchelsea.

There was an old man on whose nose
Most birds of the air could repose;
But they all flew away
At the closing of day,
Which relieved that old man and his nose.

There was an old person of Ewell,
Who chiefly subsisted on gruel;
But to make it more nice,
He inserted some mice,
Which refreshed that old person of Ewell.

There was an old man who said: "Hush!
I perceive a young bird in this bush!"
When they said: "Is it small?"
He replied: "Not at all!
It is four times as big as the bush!"

There was an old person whose habits
Induced him to feed upon rabbits;
 When he'd eaten eighteen,
 He turned perfectly green,
Upon which he relinquished those habits.

    There was an old person of Dover,
   Who rushed through a field of blue clover;
     But some very large bees
     Stung his nose and his knees,
   So he very soon went back to Dover.

There was an old man of the Wrekin,
Whose shoes made a horrible creaking;
 But they said: "Tell us whether
 Your shoes are of leather,
Or of what, you old man of the Wrekin?"

There was a young lady whose eyes
Were unique as to colour and size;
 When she opened them wide,
 People all turned aside,
And started away in surprise.

There was an Old Person of Basing
Whose presence of mind was amazing;
He purchased a steed,
Which he rode at full speed,
And escaped from the people of Basing.

There was an old bore from McRae,
Who would telephone: "What did you say?"
When assured I said nought,
He would cry: "As I thought!"
And all doubt is now taken away.

There was an old Dame of Tipperary
Who wanted to buy a canary;
When she asked: "Do you swear?"
The bird said: "I don't dare –
My behaviour is quite the contrary."

There's an Irishman, Arthur O'Shaughnessy –
On the chessboard of poets a pawn is he;
Though a bishop or king
Would be rather the thing
To the fancy of Arthur O'Shaughnessy.
DANTE GABRIEL ROSSETTI 1828–82

Twin houris who dwelt by the Bosphorus
Had eyes which shone brighter than phosphorus;
The sultan, on oath,
Cried: "I'll marry you both!"
They replied: "Oh, dear, no – you must toss for us!"

A lady while dining at Kew,
Found a fat cabbage moth in her stew;
Said the waiter: "Don't shout,
And wave it about,
Or the others will all want one too!"

There was an old man of Blackheath
Who sat on a set of false teeth;
　　Said he, with a start:
　　"Oh, Lord, bless my heart!
I have bitten myself underneath."

　　　There was a young lady of Florence
　　Who for kissing professed great abhorrence;
　　　　But when she'd been kissed,
　　　　And found what she'd missed,
　　She cried till the tears came in torrents.

There was an old Scot named McTavish
Who attempted an anthropoid ravish;
　　The object of rape
　　Was the wrong sex of ape,
And the anthropoid ravished McTavish.

　　　　　There was an old maid of Pitlochry
　　　　Whose morals were truly a mockery;
　　　　　　For, under the bed
　　　　　　Was a lover, instead
　　　　　Of the usual porcelain crockery.

The Reverend Mr Uprightly
Was cuckolded both daily and nightly;
He murmured: "Oh, dear!
I would feign interfere,
If I knew how to do it politely."

A habit obscene and unsavoury
Holds the Bishop of Wessex in slavery;
With maniacal howls
He deflowers young owls,
Which he keeps in an underground aviary.

There once was a sculptor named Phideas
Who had a distaste for the hideous;
So he "sculped" Aphrodite
Without any nightie,
And shocked all the ultra-fastidious!

A fly and a flea in a flue
Were imprisoned, but what could they do?
Said the fly: "Let us flee!"
Said the flea: "Let us fly!"
And they flew through a flaw in the flue.

There once was a pious young priest
Who lived almost wholly on yeast;
"For," he said. "it is plain
We must all rise again,
And I want to get started, at least."

There was a young lady named Perkins,
Exceedingly fond of small gherkins;
    She went out to tea,
    And ate forty-three,
Which pickled her internal workings.

Said a constable, stern, on his beat,
To a couple more fond than discreet:
    "Though a Miss miss a kiss,
    Give the next kiss a miss,
For a kiss is amiss in the street!"

There was a young lady of Crewe
Who wanted to catch the 2.02;
    Said a porter: "Don't worry,
    There's no need to hurry –
It's a minute or two to 2.02."

There was an Old Man who supposed
That the street door was partially closed;
But some very large rats
Ate his coats and his hats,
While that futile Old Gentlemen dozed.

An obstinate lady of Leicester
Wouldn't marry her swain though he pressed her;
For his income, I fear,
Was a hundred a year,
On which he could never have dressed her!

There once was a bonnie Scotch laddie
Who said as he put on his plaidie:
   "I've just had a dish
   O' unco' guid fish."
What had 'e had? He'd had haddie.

    To London there came, from Korea,
    A man with a great big left ear;
      As a blanket, at night,
      It was valuable, quite,
    But in a packed tube train – oh, dear!
              LANGFORD REED

A Jew and a Scotsman, found tight,
Were charged by a bobby one night;
   But the Judge slyly winks:
   "Where's the man who stood drinks?
He's the culprit, if I judge them right!"
H. V. ABRAHAM

    A tiger, by taste anthropophagous,
    Felt a yearning within his oesophagus;
      He spied a fat Brahmin,
      And growled: "Where's the harm in
      A peripatetic sarcophagus?"

If you wish in this world to advance,
Your merits you're bound to enhance;
You must stir it and stump it,
And blow your own trumpet,
Or, trust me, you haven't a chance!

W. S. GILBERT

A trader named Sandy MacVeetie,
With a cannibal King signed a Treaty;
In a glass of gin-sling,
MacV toasted the King,
And then the King – toasted MacVeetie!

F. J. SMITH

A patriot living at Ewell,
Found his bonfire required more fuel,
So he threw Uncle James
In the midst of the flames –
A measure effective, but cruel.

LANGFORD REED

The Reverend Henry Ward Beecher
Deemed a hen a most elegant creature;
The hen, pleased with that,
Laid an egg in his hat –
And thus did the hen reward Beecher.

A holidaymaker from Wilts
Promenaded through Scotland on stilts;
   When the locals cried: "Shocking!
   To show so much stocking."
She replied: "What of you, and your kilts!"

       An Indian maiden, a Sioux,
     As tempting as fresh honeydioux,
       Liked to show off her knees,
       As she strolled past tepees,
   And hear the braves holler: "Wioux! Wioux!"

There was an old lady of Herm
Who tied bows on the tail of a worm;
   Said she; "You look festive,
   But don't get too restive –
You'll wiggle them off if you squirm!"

A mouse in her room woke Miss Dowd.
She was frightened, it must be allowed,
   Though a clever thought hit her
   To scare off the critter;
She climbed down from her chair and meowed.

There was an Old Man of Dumbree,
Who taught little owls to drink tea;
For he said; "To eat mice
Is not proper or nice."
That amiable Man of Dumbree.

There was a young lady of Crewe
Whose eyes were excessively blue;
    She got an old fellow
    To rub them with yellow,
And so they turned green, which is true.

A bugler named Douglas MacDougal
Found ingenious ways to be frugal:
He learned how to sneeze
In different keys,
Thereby saving the price of a bugle.

There was a young lady of Ryde
Whose locks were unusually dyed;
The hue of her hair
Made everyone stare:
"She's piebald! She'll die bald!" they cried.

There was a young lady of station;
"I love man!" was her loud exclamation.
But when men cried: "You flatter!"
She answered: "No matter –
Isle of Man is the true explanation!"

Consider the lowering lynx:
He's savage, and sullen, and stynx;
Though he never has stunk
Like the scandalous skunk –
'Tis a task far beyond him, methinks.

LANGFORD REED

A slow-footed stockman called Beales
Slipped up with a bull at his heels;
When trying to rise,
He got quite a surprise,
Learning something of what a cow feels!
CYRIL MOUNTJOY

There was an old fellow of Trinity,
A doctor well versed in Divinity;
But he took to free thinking,
And then to deep drinking,
And so had to leave the vicinity.

A lovely young girl named Anne Heuser
Declared that no man could surprise her;
But a fellow named Gibbons
Untied her Blue Ribbons,
And now she is sadder Budweiser.

NB Anheuser, Gibbons, Blue Ribbons and Budweiser are the brand-names
of American beers

Limericks about Limericks

The limerick packs laughs anatomical
Into space that is quite economical;
But the good ones I've seen
So seldom are clean,
And the clean ones so seldom are comical.

The limerick form is so queasy,
It's no trick at all to be breezy;
But the lines of its wit
Are oft flavoured with shit,
Thus arousing the qualms of the queasy.

The limerick is furtive and mean;
You must keep her in strict quarantine,
Or she sneaks to the slums,
And promptly becomes
Disorderly, drunk and obscene.

LIM

There once was a bard of Hong Kong
Who thought limericks were too long.

GERARD BENSON

There was a young lady … tut, tut!
So you think that you're in for some smut?
Some five-line crescendo
Of lewd innuendo?
Well, you're wrong. This is anything but.
S. J. SHARPLESS

I'm bored to extinction with Harrison,
His limericks and puns are embarrassin';
But I'm fond of the bum,
For, though dull as they come,
He makes me feel bright by comparison.

At Harvard a randy old Dean
Said: "The funniest jokes are obscene.
To bowdlerize wit
Takes the shit out of it –
And who wants a limerick clean?

There was a young man of Japan,
Who wrote verses that never would scan;
When folk told him so,
He replied: "Yes, I know,
But I always try and get as many words into
The last line as I possibly can!"

If you find for your verse there's no call,
And you can't afford paper at all,
    For the poet, true born,
    However forlorn,
There's always the lavatory wall!

No matter how grouchy you're feeling,
You'll find that a limerick's healing;
    It grows in a wreath
    All around the front teeth,
Thus preserving the face from congealing.

Well, it's partly the shape of the thing
That gives the old limerick wing;
    Those accordion pleats,
    Full of airy conceits,
Take it up like a kite on a string.

Although at the limericks of Lear
We may feel a temptation to sneer,
We should never forget
That we owe him a debt
For his work as the first pioneer.

The limerick's callous and crude,
Its morals distressingly lewd;
It's not worth the reading
By persons of breeding –
It's designed for us vulgar and rude.

A limerick writer called Fred
Composed much of his work in his bed;
His poor wife declared
That she wouldn't have cared,
But he tapped out the beat on her head!

An inspired young writer named Dickie
Often woke feeling quite limericky;
He adored writing rhyme
Almost all of the time,
But not this morning…

With respect to the great Mr Lear,
Inventor of rhymes without peer,
His limericks are fine
Until the last line,
When the Muse seems to leave him, I fear.

These verses, one can but surmise,
Weren't intended for innocent eyes;
Should the Bishop, or Dean,
Ascertain what they mean,
They'd be sure to turn pink with surprise!

There is an anthologist who
Has decided that nought is taboo;
 Her words are so rude,
 And her verses so lewd,
I am sure they'll appeal to you!

There was a young poet from Australia
Who regarded his work as a failure;
 His verse were fine,
 Until the fourth line

Modern limerick verse is imbued
With suggestion, invariably crude;
Your fine rhymes, Mr Lear,
Are outdated, I fear,
By vocabulary risqué and rude.

A limerick writer from Bude
Concerned that his verse was too rude
 Consulted a shrink,
 And what do you think?
Now he writes all the time in the nude!

I have heard that the great Mr Lear
Drank marsala and shunned ginger beer;
    Though full to the lips, he
    Was still never tipsy,
And wrote limericks, lucid and clear.

Of limericks, Doctor Jekyll's oblivious,
Till his alter ego is delirious;
    Then it can't be denied
    Such rhymes by Mr Hyde
Will be lecherous, lewd and lascivious.

I would like to point out, Mr Lear,
That you've upset the Cornish, it's clear,
    For the town of Liskeard
    Rhymes with bard, card or hard –
Making nonsense of your rhyme I fear!

My rhymes are not bawdy or rude.
I find it quite hard to be crude,
    Or cheeky or naughty
    (I'm well over forty),
No doubt you will call me a prude.
MARY DANIELS

The limerick's an art form complex,
Whose contents run chiefly to sex;
It's famous for virgins
And masculine urgings,
And vulgar, erotic effects.

The limerick's, admitted, a verse form:
A terse form: a curse form: a hearse form.
It may not be lyric
And at best it's Satyric,
And a whale of a tail in perverse form.

There was a young man from that town in Wales
with the really long name,
Who planned to write limericks for fame;
But, try as he might,
He could not get it right,
Because nothing rhymes with
Llanfairpwllgwyngyllgogerychwyrndrobwllllantysiliogogogoch.

Though some limericks may need excusing,
Their wit is not all unamusing;
From the good and the bad,
I'd advise you, my lad,
To employ some discretion whilst choosing.

A poet, the great Rimmer-Hicks,
Would oft find himself in a fix:
He would jump up and down,
Sometimes run through the town,
Seeking endings for his... rhyming poems!

A limerick tells of a scene
Which often is crude or obscene;
    But, if smut's what you're after
    To bring about laughter,
Then tough, because this one is clean!

The poet was stuck for a rhyme.
Would he get his verse written in time?
    He thought and he thought,
    But he came up with nought –
So he chose to leave out the last line.

    Please, do not think me a prude,
    But your limericks are rather rude;
      So, could you revise,
      Or – I'll venture – excise
    Those that are especially lewd?

    There once was a fellow from Gwent
    Who wrote a short verse, and it went:
      "A fellow named Clyde
      Lived his life and then died."
    But nobody knew what it meant!

The limerick, peculiar to English,
Is a verse form that's hard to extinguish;
   Once Congress, in session,
   Decreed its suppression,
But the people got round it by writing the last
line without rhyme or rhythm.

An unfortunate naturist, Clare,
Was pursued by a large polar bear;
   I will not evoke
   That old "bear behind" joke –
This rhyme is a clean one, so there!
FRANK RICHARDS

Family Limericks

A young schizophrenic from Struther,
When told of the death of his brother,
    Said: "Yes, it's too bad,
    But I can't feel too sad –
After all, I still have each other!"

When Daddy and Mum got quite plastered,
And their shame had been thoroughly mastered,
    They told their boy Harry;
    "Son, we never did marry,
But don't tell the neighbours, you bastard!"

A lady there was in Antigua
Who told her fat spouse: "What a pigua!"
    He answered: "My queen,
    Is it manners you mean,
Or do you refer to my figua?"

A widow whose singular vice
Was to keep her late husband on ice,
    Said: "It's been hard since I lost him –
    I shall never defrost him!"
Cold comfort, but cheap at the price!

Said a fair-headed maiden of Klondike:
"Of you I'm exceedingly fond, Ike.
    To prove I adore you
    I'll dye, darling, for you,
And be a brunette, not a blonde, Ike."

Two sisters called Hetty and Heather
Wore come-hither hats in hot weather;
    A feathery trim
    Adorned each little brim,
And the girls cooed: "We're birds of a feather!"

There was a young lady of Malta
Who strangled her aunt with a halter;
    She said: "I'll not bury her,
    She'll do for my terrier –
She should keep several weeks if I salt her."

There was a young girl of Navarre
Who was frightfully fond of Jack Tar;
    When she followed him over
    From Calais to Dover,
Her relatives cried: "That's too far!"

A dentist named Archibald Moss
Fell in love with the dainty Miss Ross;
    But he held in abhorrence
    Her Christian name, Florence,
And renamed her his Dental Floss.

There was a young fellow named Hammer
Who had an unfortunate stammer;
    "The bane of my life,"
    Said he, "Is my wife,
D-d-d-d-d-d-damn her!"

A handsome young bastard called Ray
Was conceived on the Rue de la Paix;
According to law,
He can name you his ma,
But as for papa, *je ne sais*.

There was a young fellow named Hyde
Who fell in a privy and died;
His unfortunate brother
Fell into another,
And now they're interred side by side.

A schoolgirl with homework (distraught),
Got her father to do it. She thought
That his skill was far greater,
But she wept a week later –
Dad's mark out of ten? It was nought.

They've buried a salesman named Phipps.
He got married on one of his trips
To a widow named Block,
But he died of the shock
When he found there were six little chips.

A dentist who lives in Duluth
Has wedded a widow named Ruth;
She is so sentimental
Concerning things dental,
She calls her dear second her twoth.

A herder who hailed from Terre Haute,
Fell in love with a young nanny goat;
The daughter he sired
Was greatly admired
For her beautiful angora coat.

A middle-aged lady of Condover,
Had a husband who'd ceased to be fond of her;
He could not forget
He had wooed a brunette,
But peroxide had since made a blonde of her.

Said a gleeful young bounder from Bray:
"This is rather a red-letter day!
For I've poisoned, with sherbert,
My rich Uncle Herbert,
Whose health showed no signs of decay."

A man of a hundred-and-three
Dived every day into the sea;
When they said: "Are you mad?"
He replied: "It's my dad –
He insists on fresh herrings for tea!"

A husband who lived in Tiberias,
Once laughed himself almost delirious;
But he laughed at his wife,
Who took up a sharp knife
With results that were quite deleterious.

There was an old spinster from Fife
Who had never been kissed in her life;
   Along came a cat,
   And she said: "I'll kiss that!"
But the cat meowed: "Not on your life!"

     "Always take care of your head,"
    The ghost of my Granny once said,
      "While it's under your arm,
       It can come to no harm,
    But at night put it under the bed."

In Summer he said she was fair,
And in Autumn her charms were still there;
   But he said to his wife
   In the Winter of life:
"There's no Spring in your old derriere!"

There was a young lady called Millicent
Who hated the perfume that Willie sent;
   So she sent it to Liz
   Who declared: "What a swizz –
It's that silly scent Willie sent Millicent!"

An amoeba named Sam, and his brother,
Were having a drink with each other;
In the midst of their quaffing,
They split themselves laughing,
And each of them now is a mother!

Said a pretty young girl: "I shall smother
That nasty young twerp of a brother;
I've just heard him say
I'll be fifty next May,
And he's told all his mates I'm his *mother*!"

There was an old fellow of Clewer
Whose wife was as thin as a skewer;
Last night, sad to say,
She, at eight, passed away,
Through the bars of a drain to the sewer.

There once was a schoolboy named Hannibal
Who won local fame as a cannibal,
By eating his mother,
His father, his brother,
And his two sisters, Gertrude and Annabelle.

There was a young lady from Gloster,
Whose parents believed they had lost her;
From the fridge came a sound,
And, at last, she was found,
The problem was – how to defrost her?

My dad whose as bald as a bat,
Spilt hair tonic over the mat;
Now it's grown so much higher,
You can't see the fire,
And we've searched it in vain for the cat!

There was a young girl from Furness
Who invited a friend to play chess;
But she'd lent half the pieces
To one of her nieces,
And couldn't recall the address.

I once took my girl to Great Bend,
Intending a loving weekend;
But imagine the fuss –
In the room next to us
Was my wife with a gentleman friend.
VERONICA NICOLSON

A boy who was known as a gadabout,
Was boasting away to his dad about
    His conquest of lasses;
    Dad said: "You need glasses –
There's nowt in that lot to go mad about!"

    So obese is my cousin from Hendon,
    She looks elephantine, viewed end on;
        What preys most on her mind
        Are her efforts to find
    A good deck-chair that she can depend on.
A.H. BAYNES

Said newlywed, hen-pecked MacLeod:
"I wish that two wives were allowed,
    I've discovered that one
    Is a son-of-a-gun,
Although three, I am told, is a crowd!"

    There was an old lady of Rye
    Who was baked by mistake in a pie;
        To the family's disgust,
        She broke out through the crust,
    And exclaimed, with a yawn: "Where *am* I?"

A youthful beef-packer named Young,
One day, when his nerves were unstrung,
    Pushed his wife's ma (unseen)
    In the chopping machine,
Then canned her, and labelled her "Tongue".

    My sister, Penelope Pinner
    Grows steadily thinner and thinner;
        The reason is plain:
        She sleeps out in the rain,
    And is never allowed any dinner.

A precocious young lady named Lillian
Stuck out her pink tongue at a Chilean;
    Her mother said, pleading:
    "Remember your breeding –
That habit's distinctly reptilian!"

A Canadian woodsman named Weaver
Has a wife with a face like a beaver;
    Her sharp teeth, with ease,
    Will cut down large trees –
So there's no way poor Weaver can leave her.

"Look at this!" said a lady named Mabel,
Doing tricks upside down on the table;
When her son screamed out: "Mother!"
She replied: "Here's another."
Grabbed the light and swung up by the cable.

There was an old widower, Doyle,
Who wrapped up his wife in tinfoil;
He thought it would please her
To stay in the freezer,
And, anyway – outside she'd spoil!

A chap and his ladylove Min,
Skating out where the ice was so thin,
Had a quarrel, no doubt,
For I hear they fell out,
They were lucky they didn't fall in!

A pregnant young girl from Fort Worth
Was so shy of her increasing girth;
But sadly her figure
Got bigger and bigger,
And bigger and bigger – till birth.

"If she ever gets caught in the rain,"
Cried the mother of slimming-mad Jane,
"I can picture her fate –
She has lost so much weight,
Mark my words, she'll get washed down a drain!"

Great Grandfather, at Waterloo,
Fought solidly all the day through;
   He slashed and he hacked
   Through the bodies, tight-packed,
And he managed to reach Platform Two.
FRANK RICHARDS

Widow (conscious that time's on the wing),
Fortyish, but still game for a fling,
   Seeks fun-loving male,
   Mature, but not stale,
With a view to the usual thing.
S. J. SHARPLESS

There was an Old Person of Looe
   Who said: "What on earth shall I do?"
   When they said: "Go away!"
She continued to stay,
That vexacious Old Person of Looe.

There was an old miser named Clarence
Who simonized both of his parents;
   "The initial expense,"
He remarked, "Is immense,
But I'll save it in wearance and tearance!"

There was a young fellow from Boone
Who howled like a wolf at the moon;
   His mum found it scary
   When he grew so hairy,
But hoped he'd get over it soon.

There is a young lady from Splott
Who has to put up with a lot;
   Her husband's a pain,
   And her kids are the same,
But does she complain? She does not.

                    Uncle Bill used to play ukulele,
                    Thus annoying his relatives daily,
                        Above all his daughter,
                        On trial for manslaughter
                    Next week, in Court One, the Old Bailey.

There was a punk rocker from Tring
Who embellished his nose with a ring;
   His wife said: "That's fine,
   You behave like a swine –
So you might as well look the real thing!"
FRANK RICHARDS

Captain Hook was not pleased with his lot.
He regrets ever tying the knot;
He's buried his "treasure",
His wife (gone forever) –
An appropriate "ex" marks the spot!

REG LYNES

An out-of-work clown from Caerphilly
Complained to his wife: "Dearest Lily –
It's tough being idle;
I feel suicidal."
She said: "Please, don't do anything silly!"

RON RUBIN

An insensitive chap from South Park
Made an unnecessary remark;
　He said: "Aunty Flo,
　I am dying to know –
Tell me, what was life like in the Ark?"

My Auntie is one of those women
Who's always on diets, and slimming;
Said she: "Till I lose
Three stone, I refuse
To take off my clothes and go swimming!"

There was an old woman named Doris
Who married a duffer called Boris;
When Doris and Boris
Produced little Norris,
They opened a florist in Corris.

When Tommy first met Uncle Pete
(Now Tommy is five and can speak),
He said: "Auntie Rose,
Does he put on his nose
The same stuff you paint on your cheeks?"

A cute, bonny baby of yore,
Was as big as a flea, little more;
Its parents, afraid
That it might be mislaid,
Have stored it away in a drawer.

There was an old woman of Churston
Who thought her third husband the worst 'un;
For he rightly was reckoned
Far worse than the second,
And her second was worse than the first 'un.

Oh, daddy, may I marry soon?
I love him. I'm over the moon!
What? Could I delay
Till April, or May?
But you'll be a granddad by June!

There was a man in Henderson
Who had a tall and slender son:
A human rail
Who used a nail
To fasten his suspenders on.

The young couple who lived at "The Laurels"
Had the most unbelievable morals;
You'll not view in a zoo
What those two got up to,
Making up when they'd had lovers' quarrels!

Three Aldis, not one of them dim,
Were Garib and Fresco and Grim;
One played and one clowned,
And the other's renowned
By a biscuit that's named after him!
JOYCE JOHNSON

The sisters next door – the Miss Evanses,
Have poisoned their mother's elevenses;
Without her on her feet,
There is nothing to eat,
And the house is at sixes and sevenses!

A philanderer, living in Bow,
Not the ideal acquaintance to know,
Kept ten wives (more or less)
At his city address,
And several more in a small bungalow.
FRANK RICHARDS

Fat William, whose manners aren't good,
Was asked if he'd like some more pud;
He cried: "Yes!" on the spot,
Said his mother: "Yes, what?"
And young Billy replied: "Yes, I would!"

"There's a face at the window." said Pat.
Said his mum: "What's so odd about that?"
"Well, I find it rum,"
Said the lad to his mum,
"Since we live in an eighteenth-floor flat!"

A knight with a wife called Eliza
Kissed her one afternoon to surprise her;
   He did that all right,
   But he gave her a fright –
He'd forgotten to take off his visor!

A learned professor from Fyfe
Who has lived in a dream all his life,
As a matter of course,
Will cuddle his horse,
Then run out and saddle his wife!

My parrot's a wonderful bird,
But the situation's becoming absurd:
   It spends all its life
   Contradicting my wife,
And, between them, I can't say a word!
J. JACKSON

Twin sisters I know – the Hall-Daces,
Used to go in for three-legged races;
Once, an onlooker cried:
"I believe I've just spied
A girl with three legs and two faces!"

His Dad said: "You're bone idle, Bob!
It's time you were getting a job."
Bob yawned: "I'm too proud
To consort with the crowd –
It's not laziness, I'm just a snob!"

FRANK RICHARDS

A bearded old bounder called Morse
Quite fanatic for all things Norse,
Found that going to bed,
Viking helmet on head,
Only led to an early divorce!

An Italian lady named Vera
Has saved millions and millions of lire;
She wants a small house
For herself and her spouse,
But they keep getting dearer and dearer.

REG LYNES

"I've made out my Will," said old Waters,
As he gazed at his four weeping daughters;
"I'm leaving to you
My pet cockatoo –
Divide it up, please, into quarters…"

RON RUBIN

"Now Len, you're an artistic lad,
So why don't you paint me?" said dad;
So, without more ado,
Len painted Dad – blue!
And Dad, I might add, is quite mad…

Said Bert, who's a bit of a wally:
"Now, what could I buy for my Molly?"
He pondered for hours,
Then said: "I know – flowers!"
And the next day he gave her a cauli!

An astronomer christened Carruthers
Announced to his dumbfounded brothers:
"These pickles in jars,
Did you know , came from Mars?"
What he meant was – they came from his mother's.

A bigamist, name of McGraw,
Was freed by the High Court: "For sure."
Said the judge, with a grin,
"You have paid for your sin,
By having two mother's-in-law!"

"I've shut my wife up in this box,"
Said an old chap, securing the locks.
"For years now," said he,
"She's said 'Shut Up' to me –
So, how's that for a nice paradox!"

FRANK RICHARDS

There was a professor of Botany
Whose wife sighed: "My life is monotony –
   The trees, shrubs and flowers
   You study for hours,
But, sometimes, I think you've forgotten *me*!"
RON RUBIN

An old chap from St Michaels-on-Wyre
Turned his thermostat higher and higher;
   Till one very cold night,
   His poor wife had a fright,
When he fled with his jim-jams on fire!

          Said Eve, with a sniff of disgust:
    "Who could lust for a man made of dust?"
          Said Adam: "Distrust her!
          She'll soon find a duster –
    A housewife is never nonplussed."

          A big bouncing baby called Brett
        Discovered he'd got soaking wet;
          "The secret of happiness
         Is nice, warm, dry nappiness."
      He observed, with a hint of regret.

A baby in Kalamazoo
Remarked, quite distinctly: "Goo. Goo!"
   'Twas explained by his ma,
   And likewise his pa,
That he'd meant to say: "How do you do?"

Children's Limericks

FOR CHILDREN AND BY CHILDREN

LIMERICKS FOR CHILDREN

A young engine driver at Crewe
Stuck his old chewing gum in the flue;
A boy passing by,
Remarked: "I know why
The engine says chew-chew, chew-chew!"

There was a young chap from Eugene
Who grew so abnormally lean,
And flat and compressed,
That his back met his chest,
And, viewed sideways, he couldn't be seen!

A sea serpent saw a big tanker,
Bit a hole in its side and then sank her;
He swallowed the crew
In a minute or two,
And then picked his teeth with the anchor.

Consider the poor hippopotamus:
His life is unduly monotonous;
He lives half-asleep
At the edge of the deep,
And his face is as big as his bottom is.

A small group of schoolgirls from Grays
Got lost in the Hampton Court Maze,
Where each reprobate child
Regressed to the wild,
Surviving on squirrel for days!

There was a young lady of Wilts
Who strode through the highlands on stilts;
   When they cried: "Oh, how shocking
   To reveal so much stocking!"
She replied: "Ah, but what about kilts?"

There was an old man of Peru
Who dreamt he was eating a shoe;
   He awoke in the night
   With a terrible fright,
And found it was perfectly true!

A couple of fellows from Woking
Who'd never enjoyed a good soaking,
   When told that real fellers
   Don't carry umbrellas,
Cried: "What! You have got to be joking!"

There was a young bather from Bewes,
Who reclined on the bank of the Ouse;
   His radio blared,
   And passers-by stared,
For all he had on was the news!

THE OOZILY WOOZILY PLONK

There's the Hairily Scarily Donk,
And the Heavily Devily Conk;
But none is as weird
Or so horribly feared
As the Oozily Woozily Plonk.

He likes nothing more than a chat,
But I'd strongly advise against that!
Just get on your bike,
Because you wouldn't like
What the Plonk means by "chewing the fat".

It is awfully bad manners, I know,
But just make your excuses and go;
No, don't even smile,
Run a four-minute mile
If a Plonk says as much as "Hello!"

Should a Plonk ever hunt you and find you,
He'd certainly crush you and grind you;
But there's nothing to fear,
There are none around here...
GOOD HEAVENS! THERE'S ONE
RIGHT BEHIND YOU!!
COLIN MCNAUGHTON

There once was an organic leek
That had managed to learn how to speak;
At the sight of a knife,
It would fear for its life,
And go: Eeeeeeeeeeeeeeeeeeeeeek!

JOHN HEGLEY

There's a small place in Wales called The Mumbles
That is filled with such groans and such grumbles;
    The locals complain
    Of the constant, cold rain
Which produces a coastline that crumbles.

Mr Hullabaloo went to bed in a shoe,
And he travelled around by balloon;
He wore a tall hat,
And he kept a pink cat,
And played snap with The Man in the Moon.

MARIAN SWINGER

Winnifred Gristle could whistle through thistles.
At whistling through thistles our Winn was a dream;
    No-one out-whistled
    The winsome Miss Gristle –
Winnifred Gristle, the whistler supreme.

GARETH OWEN

There are men in the village of Erith
Whom nobody seeth or heareth;
    They spend hours afloat
    In a flat-bottomed boat,
Which nobody roweth or steereth.

ADVICE FOR SPACEMEN

When you test your rocket,
Oil the engine sprocket
Which none replace
In Outer Space;
Shops up there don't stock it.

When you fly your rocket,
Time your flight and clock it;
Don't exceed
Hyperspeed.
Safety first. Don't mock it.

When you park your rocket,
Do watch where you dock it;
The Spaceway Code
Says; off the road.
Otherwise, you block it.

When you mend your rocket,
Don't hammer it or knock it;
Just read the rules
On robot tools,
Then plug them in the socket.

When you leave your rocket,
Don't forget to lock it;
The only place
For keys in Space
Is in your trouser pocket.

NICK TOCZEK

MISS MUFFET

There was a young girl called Miss Muffet
Who sat down one day on a tuffet;
She'd sooner have had
A chair, I might add,
But sometimes you just have to rough it.

She was scoffing her curds and her whey,
When a spider came up and said: "Hey!
I know this sounds hackneyed,
But I'm an arachnid
Alone – may I lunch with you, pray?"

As she shrugged and made room on her tuffet,
He whooped: "You're my lunch, dear Miss Muffet!"
Then the monstrous tarantula
Began to dismantle her,
And that's how Miss M came to snuff it.

RON RUBIN

The foolish girl was wrong enough,
And had to wait quite long enough;
For as she sat,
She grew so fat
That nobody was strong enough!

THE DAUGHTER OF THE FARRIER

The daughter of the farrier
Could find no-one to marry her,
Because she said
She would not wed
A man who could not carry her.

Two brothers called Reggie and Fred
Chased a fierce-looking wasp from their bed;
Said Fred: "It's gone. How?"
Said Reg: "Don't look now –
But it's sitting on top of your head!"

I've eaten as much as I can,
I cannot digest one more gram;
I'm leaving the chips,
And the salady bits,
And the peas, and the egg, and the ham!
REG LYNES

A sporty young fellow named Yonkers
Spent all his spare time playing conkers;
One afternoon (tut!),
He cracked his *own* nut –
And ended up stark raving bonkers!

There was a young girl from Caerphilly
Who finds it exceedingly chilly;
It isn't that Wales
Has such extra cold vales,
But the fact that it's also quite hilly.
MARGARET BRACE

Said a testy old gentleman: "Why
Should this fly in my eye try to die?
    If bent on its doom,
    Why should it assume
There is room for its tomb in my eye?"

A tough guy who lived in the West,
Was shot sixty times in the chest;
    He said: "It don't hurt,
    But it's ruined my shirt,
And I'm certain to need a new vest!"

An indisciplined child called McLunday
Always got to school late, until one day
    He was early for once,
    But the ignorant dunce
Had forgotten that it was a Sunday!

Said a school dinner-lady called Sweet:
    "I am giving up maths, in defeat;
    I was sure a square root
    Was a tropical fruit,
And that Pi was a nice thing to eat!"

A greedy young schoolboy called Mark
Stuffed bananas all week, for a lark;
And when he had done,
Gobbled nuts by the ton –
Now he swings through the trees in the park.

There's many a computer geek
Who could tap-tap but not really speak;
Along comes MSN,
Now they're talking again
In a series of taps, and a squeak.

MARGARET BRACE

A flighty young lady from Deal
Imagined that she was a seal;
But friends said: "We wish
She'd stop honking for fish,
As, frankly, it fails to appeal!"

MARIAN SWINGER

I've studied the stars, big and bright,
That glow in the sky every night;
What puzzles me though,
Is how do they glow –
If there's nobody there with a light?

I have an Alsatian named Rover:
His party piece? The Bossanova;
Although my pet cat
Cannot equal that,
She knits an accomplished pullover!

GREAT GINNEL GRINNER

Beware of the Great Ginnel Grinner,
It lurks where the passage gets thinner;
It stumbles and stutters,
It gropes from the gutters,
And mutters and utters – the sinner!

Beware of the Great Ginnel Grinner,
Especially as daylight grows dimmer;
It waits to inspect us,
And licks us and pecks us,
And saves bits for breakfast – and dinner!

GINA DOUTHWAITE

A robber named Brian McGrew
Decided to burgle a zoo;
But he foolishly nicked a
Huge boa constrictor
Which ate him without more ado!

An upper-crust wally named Willy
Decided to do something silly;
"I'm building a folly!"
"Oh, golly! How jolly!"
Cried Molly and Dolly and Billy.

A hamster called Septimus Claw
Leapt out of his cage to the floor;
  He wasn't to know
  That the cat lurked below –
Sadly, Septimus Claw is no more!

A ladybird lost a black spot:
"My seventh spot I have not got!"
  But the ladybird's mother
  Cried: "Splat! There's another!"
And painted a blot from a pot.
MARY DANIELS

Archaeologists dig at their leisure,
And it gives them a great deal of pleasure,
Not to mention bad backs,
As they fill up their sacks
With all sorts of muddy old treasure.

MARGARET BRACE

There was an old Prophet called Jonah
Who set sail in a ship from Ancona;
  One day, in a gale,
  He was ate by a whale,
And sicked up on the beach in a coma.
DICKIE DUNN

BULLY BOY McCOY

I'm Bully Boy McCoy, ahoy!
An' bein' a bully's what I enjoy
I'll bully thee
If yer smaller'n me,
I'm Bully Boy McCoy, ahoy!

I'm Bully Boy McCoy, avast!
Hand o'er yer treasure an' make it fast!
I'm hard as nails,
I never fails!
I'm Bully Boy McCoy, avast!

I'm Bully Boy McCoy, ooh-arrgh!
I navigates by sun an' by star.
An' stealin' treasure?
That's me pleasure!
I'm Bully Boy McCoy, ooh-arrgh!

I'm Bully Boy McCoy, I be!
I'm sailing home to have me tea.
I'm in a state,
Cos if I'm late –
My mummy will be cross with me!
COLIN MCNAUGHTON

Two dinosaurs strolling. arms linked,
Met a little old lady who blinked,
   And said, in surprise,
   Whilst rubbing her eyes:
"They told me that you were extinct!"
MARIAN SWINGER

A jolly old fellow in red
Set his reindeer on full-speed ahead;
   And all in one night,
   Much faster than light,
Left presents round everyone's bed!
MARIAN SWINGER

There once was a woman of Gwent
Who was useless at pitching a tent;
   She hammered a peg
   Through a bone in her leg,
And immediately after, she went:
Aaaaaaaaaaaargh!
JOHN HEGLEY

A prickly old gardener called Ted
Grew such champion roses (deep red);
   The Show Judge said: "Poor you,
   Your blooms should be blue!"
Now he's growing potatoes instead.

The double-bass boom of the bittern,
Once common across much of Britain,
Is now seldom heard.
This endangered bird's
As rare as a poem well written.
NICK TOCZEK

A visitor from Outer Space
On arriving presented his case:
  "Earthlings? Inferior!
  My race? Superior!"
Tripped up and fell flat on his face.

A man who'd spent years on the roads,
Driving lorries with extra-wide loads,
Never ever felt bad
That his Michelins had
Flattened thousands of natterjack toads.

An unfortunate schoolboy called Pete
Had extremely malodorous feet;
  If he waggled one sock,
  The olfactory shock
Could empty the average street!
MARIAN SWINGER

There was an old fellow from Pinner
Whose wife became thinner and thinner;
  He told her: "My dear,
  You'll soon disappear –
Stop slimming, start eating your dinner!"
CATHERINE OSBORNE

There's a chap who's quite happy to boast
That his mouth is much bigger than most;
　　For breakfast he usually
　　Has buckets of muesli
And hundreds of slices of toast!

A little old granny called Maud
Got stuck in a ford in a Ford;
　　The RAC man
　　Arrived in his van,
And observed: "Dearie me! Oh, gor blimey! My gawd!"

As they fished his crashed plane from the sea,
The inventor just chortled with glee:
　　"I shall fashion," he laughed,
　　"A submarine craft,
And perhaps it will fly, we shall see!"

There was an old gnu in the Zoo
Who tired of the same daily view;
　　To seek a new sight,
　　He broke out one night,
But where he went, gnobody gnew!

There was an old dame of Malacca
Who smoked such obnoxious tobacca,
　　That, when tigers came near,
　　They trembled with fear,
And didn't attempt to attacka.

An elephant never forgets,
Neither messages, shopping nor debts;
He can hold in his trunk
A whole cartload of junk –
And the little ones make super pets!

"What," said our teacher, Miss Pink,
"Is this moth doing here in my ink?"
Said a cheeky young lass,
At the front of the class:
"Butterfly Stroke, I should think!"

There's a witch in our village called Joyce
Who is cursed with a hideous voice;
But, please, don't assume
She rides round on a broom –
She's rich, and she drives a Rolls Royce!

At school we have big books of reference,
That teacher regards with great deference;
But encyclopaedias
Do get rather tedious –
Comics are really *my* preference!

A naughty young schoolboy from Datchet
Sneaked off with his grandfather's hatchet;
Then was heard to cry: "Oh!
I've chopped off my toe!
Won't somebody please re-attach it?"

"How d'you spell Xmas?" asked Bess –
The new teacher was trying to assess
Her pupils' grey matter,
When she heard, through the chatter:
"Is it E-C-Z-E-M-A-S?"
RON RUBIN

There's a miserable author who tries
Every method to economize;
He'll say, with a wink:
"I save gallons of ink,
By simply not dotting my 'i's'!"

In a nightmare, a boy called Ron Meeking,
Was drowning and rescue was seeking;
Then he woke up, and yet,
His pyjamas were wet –
His hot water bottle was leaking!

LIMERICKS BY CHILDREN

Thr wnce ws a grl frm SX
Who cdnt stp usin hr txt;
She ws gtin a bor,
I cud nt take no mor,
So I fd hr phn 2 my dg Rx.
VIOLET MACDONALD (13)

My jumper was smart though not posh,
And it cost Mum a good deal of dosh;
The colours were bright,
And it wasn't too tight,
But, sadly, it's shrunk in the wash.
CELINA MACDONALD (15)

I knew an old guy from Ukraine,
So posh he threw dosh down the drain,
And some in a ditch;
But he's no longer rich –
Now he begs on the streets in the rain.
CELINA MACDONALD (15)

When the hugely-popular children's television programme, Blue Peter, announced a limerick competition, over 8,000 entries were received within a matter of weeks. Here is a selection of the winning verses:

There once was a programme, Blue Peter,
Asked for limericks with plenty of metre;
They arrived host by host,
Inundating the post,
And buried poor John, Val and Peter.*

*John, Val and Peter were the programme's presenters at the time

There was a young lad called Davy
Who hated the food in the Navy;
    He couldn't have beef
    In case his false teeth
Would drop out and fall in the gravy.
RAYMOND COLEMAN (11)

There is a young boxer named Walter,
Who comes from the island of Malta;
    One day in the ring
    He stepped on a spring,
And bounced all the way to Gibraltar.
DAVID MCDERMOTT (13)

There was a young cannibal, Ned,
Who used to eat onions in bed;
   His mother said: "Sonny,
   It's not very funny –
Why don't you eat people instead?"
GILLIAN NASH (11)

A hungry old goat named Heather
Was tied up with an old bit of leather;
   In a minute or two
   She had chewed it right through,
And that was the end of her tether!
CELIA MCMASTER (12)

There is a maths teacher called Rundle
Who ties up his books in a bundle;
   It's too heavy he feels,
   So he's put it on wheels –
Now Rundle can trundle his bundle!
AMANADA CHEW (13)

My brother's name is Keith:
He hates to clean his teeth;
   His dirty face
   Is a real disgrace,
But he's lovely underneath!
BRIAN BELL (5)

There was a young fellow called Fred
Had an elephant sit on his head;
Where the elephant sat,
Fred's head grew quite flat,
But Fred didn't care, he was dead!

AUDREY FREELAND (12)

There was a young girl called Pam
Who turned up her nose at some ham;
But, when offered some cheese,
She would say: "Oh, yes please,
Though I'm slimming as much as I can!"

KATHERINE SAUNDERS (10)

A certain young fellow called Peter
Went out to buy oil for his heater;
He asked for a quart,
But the man said: "You ought
To know that it's bought by the litre!"

CLAIRE ALLEN (11)

There was an old teacher named Brass
Who was blessed with an unbrainy class;
They slept and they snored,
And completely ignored
Theorems like "Pythagoras".

SUSAN OWENS (15)

There was a young man with a horse,
A very keen rider, of course;
He tried to jump over
The White Cliffs of Dover,
But couldn't quite muster the force.
ALISON LYNE (9)

There was a young laddie called Tony
Who ate plates of fried macaroni;
He got very fat,
But he didn't mind that,
'Cos he bounced when he sat on his pony.
BELINDA KELLETT (8)

A certain young goalie called Finn
Lost count of the goals he let in;
When his skipper bawled: "Eight!"
He replied, quite sedate:
"Then we only need nine goals to win!"
MARK ROTHERY (8)

There was a poor moggie from Hyde
Who heard that next door's dog had died;
He went through the gate,
Met a terrible fate,
'Cos the cat that had told him had lied!
RICHARD BOOTH (11)

There was a young man of Arbroath
Who kept for a pet a large sloth;
He said; "It's quite nice,
But it doesn't like mice,
So I buy fish and chips for us both!"

DEBORAH WESTOVER (11)

There was a composer called Strauss
Who lived with a cat and a mouse;
Said Johann one day:
"I am glad they can stay."
So they all did a waltz round the house.
PATRICK HAYWARD (6)

There was a brown dog called Spot
Who tied up his tail with a knot,
To remember his bone
Which he'd left back at home
When he sometimes went out for a trot.
REBECCA TELFORD (7)

There was a young fellow from Crewe
Who'd been a royalist since he was two;
When he found grass was green,
He cried: "God save the Queen!"
And painted it red, white and blue.
CLARE SIMMONS (13)

There was a young lady of Leeds
Who was constantly doing good deeds;
As she bit her young brother,
She said to her mother:
"I'll bind up the wound if it bleeds!"
CHRISTINE TAILBY (7)

Food and Drink Limericks

A poor guy from near Winnemucca
Had such an unfortunate stutter;
"I would like," he once said,
"Some b-b-b-bread,
And also some b-b-b-b-butter."

When sipping a cup of Darjeeling,
I observed that the brew was congealing;
It set like meringue,
Then went off with a bang!
And I found myself stuck to the ceiling.

A glutton who came from the Rhine
Was asked at what hour he would dine;
He replied: "At eleven,
At four, five and seven,
And eight, *and* a quarter to nine!"

There was an old biddy from Ryde
Who ate some green apples and died;
The apples fermented
Within the lamented –
Making cider inside her inside.

When you visit the store in Ascutney
There is no point in ordering chutney;
You may fall to your knees,
But your impassioned pleas
Will just fall on deaf ears – they ain't gotney!

A lady, invited to dinner,
Returned looking thin (if not thinner);
Said she: "Be not baffled,
The dinner was raffled,
And (you've guessed it) I wasn't the winner!"

There was an old man of Calcutta
Who coated his tonsils with butter,
    Thus converting his snore
    From a thunderous roar
To a soft oleagenous mutter.
OGDEN NASH

As the natives got ready to serve
A midget explorer named Merv,
    "This meal will be brief,"
    Said the cannibal chief,
"For this is at best an *hors d'oeuvre*."
ED CUNNINGHAM

It's a nightmare that horrifies hakes:
To finish as frugal fish-cakes;
    But oh, what a dream
    To be stewed, slowly in cream,
Or fresh-fried as respectable steaks.
ALLEN M. LAING

There was a young fellow named Sydney
Who drank till he ruined his kidney;
It shrivelled and shrank
As he sat there and drank –
But he had a good time of it, didn'e?

DON MARQUIS

A sensitive girl called O'Neill
Had a ride on the fairground Big Wheel;
But halfway around,
She looked down at the ground,
And it cost her a three-fifty meal.

There was a young girl from Uttoxeter,
Who worked nine-to-five as a choc-setter;
She rolled the chocs thin
With a wee rolling-pin,
So they'd fit in the After Eight box better.

S. J. SHARPLESS

An epicure living at Gratz
Was exceedingly partial to cats;
He relished them toasted,
Or boiled, or roasted,
Or thoroughly stewed in old hats.

There's a lady in Kalamazoo
Who bites all her oysters in two;
She has a misgiving
Should any be living
They would raise such a hullabaloo.

In the dark, dismal days of December,
It is always a joy to remember
That, come Christmas Day,
You'll have (hip, hip, hooray!)
A turkey, trussed up, to dismember.

A lady from Louth with a lisp
Liked her sausages specially crisp;
But in trying to say
That she liked them that way,
She covered her friends in a mitht.
MICHAEL PALIN

There was a young person named Perkins
Exceedingly fond of small gherkins;
One Summer at tea,
He ate eighty-three,
Which pickled his internal workings.

There was a young lady called Flynn
Who was so uncommonly thin,
    That, when she essayed
    To drink lemonade,
She slipped through the straw and fell in.

There was an old lady of Brooking
Who had a great talent for cooking;
    She could bake sixty pies,
    Each one quite the same size,
And yet tell which was which without looking!

An oyster from Kalamazoo
Confessed he was feeling quite blue;
    "For," he said "As a rule,
    When the weather's this cool,
I invariably get into a stew!"

An Italian chap, Valentino
Whose appetite was quite obsceno,
    Filled up-a his belly
    With tagliatelle,
And several bottles of vino!

A man of odd tastes, Mr Walton,
Would always eat mutton with malt on;
He had cheese in his coffee,
And soap with his toffee,
And spoonfuls of honey with salt on.

An eccentric old chap from Herne Bay
Lived on garlic and decomposed hay;
He said: "Though the smell
Often makes me unwell,
It does keep the midges away!"

To his wife wrote old lag Fingers Cotton:
"My darling, I haven't forgotten
Your lovely blue eyes,
And your veal and ham pies –
Them most as the grub here is rotten!"

A ravenous diner named Sid
Who ate sixty-five eggs in Madrid;
When asked: "Are you faint?"
Replied: "No, I ain't,
But I don't feel as well as I did."

A clever young farmer named Binns
Fed his cows on scrap metal and pins;
It was always the same –
When milking-time came,
It was neatly delivered in tins!

FRANK RICHARDS

A fellow who lived on the Tyne
Saw some fish on which he wished to dine;
But how to invite them?
He thought: "I shall write them!"
And sat down and dropped them a line.

A mermaid who swims off St Ives
Is unsettling the fishermen's wives;
Their plan is to net her,
Or otherwise get her,
And poach her in cream sauce with chives.

REG LYNES

A cheese that was aged and grey,
Was walking and talking one day;
Said the cheese: "Kindly note
My mamma was a goat,
And I'm made out of curds, by the whey!"

Quite the daftest that Nature could pick
Was the nanny in charge of young Nick;
She fed him mince pies,
Chocolate, ice-cream, and fries,
Then complained when the poor kid was sick!

A greengrocer's wife, named Yvette,
Took her cantaloupes out (for a bet);
A couple of felons
Made off with her melons,
And they've not apprehended them yet!
CHARLOTTE MCBEE

A particular chappie named Marvin
Was daydreaming of turkeys (and carving);
When his mum offered Spam,
He said: "No, thank you, ma'am,
I prefer the alternative – starving!"

As it sat on its holly-trimmed plate,
Said the Christmas Pud: "Don't I look great!"
Said the Sauce: "Pud, I fear,
Looks won't get you far here –
Just like me, you'll get eaten, old mate!"

A remorseful young glutton named Jake
Had incredibly bad stomach ache;
He flopped in a chair,
Saying: "It's only fair –
I wolfed the entire chocolate cake!"

Here's a diet that appears heaven-sent
(I don't know where my slim figure went);
    I must say my goodbyes
    To those burgers and fries –
And eat nothing but fast food for Lent!
CHARLOTTE MCBEE

A gardener who once lived in Harrow
Grew the world's biggest vegetable marrow;
    But, when harvest time came,
    Although it brought fame,
It completely destroyed his wheelbarrow.

Our butcher wastes no scrap of meat,
From sheep's heads to pigs trotters (that's feet);
    He puts it in pies,
    With offal and eyes –
One of which should see you through the week.
REG LYNES

A starter, a main course, a sweet,
Is sufficient for one man to eat;
    Please, no more banoffee,
    Liqueurs, or coffee –
I've had quite enough, I'm replete!

A health-concious type from Tyne Tees,
With a passion for strange herbal teas,
    Collected great sprigs
    Of leaf debris, and twigs,
And prepared an infusion of trees.
CHARLOTTE MCBEE

A missionary, I once heard tell,
Thought: "These cannibals I'll save from hell!"
    Well, they didn't care
    For the Bible, or prayer –
Though at dinner he went down quite well!

Marco Polo returned from Peking,
Bringing wonderful treasures with him:
    The first printing block,
    Gunpowder to shock,
And that pasta like long bits of string!

I went on a flight out to Tresco,
Intending to picnic alfresco;
    There were no sausage rolls,
    Or profiteroles,
So I flew home and popped into Tesco.

There's a gluttonous chap in New York,
Whose most favourite food is roast pork;
   But, hard as he tries,
   To increase his mouth size,
Only one pig will fit on his fork!

An incautious young gourmet called Shaun,
Ate a well-past-its-sellby-date prawn;
   He emitted a scream,
   Turned viridian green,
And threw up from dusk until dawn.

At last I've seduced the *au pair*
With some steak and a chocolate éclair,
   Some peas and some chips,
   Three Miracle Whips,
And a carafe of *vin ordinaire*
CYRIL RAY

At a bistro, a chap named O'Reilly,
Said: "I've heard these martinis praised highly,
   But they're better, by far,
   At a neighbouring bar,
Where they're mixed much more smoothly and dryly!"

An accomplished old baker named Fred
(Though success never went to his head),
   Instead of just looking,
   Ate all his own cooking,
And it went to his waistline instead.

A careless explorer named Blake
Fell into a tropical lake;
Said a fat alligator,
A few minutes later:
"Very nice, but I much prefer steak."

OGDEN NASH

There was an old man in a trunk
Who inquired of his wife: "Am I drunk?"
She replied, with regret:
"I'm afraid so, my pet."
And he answered: "It's just as I thunk."

OGDEN NASH

A small café outside Bowling Green
Has an owner so stingy and mean;
"If a sandwich," she said,
"Has but one slice of bread –
There's no need for a filling between!"

There once was a very old gnu
Who was used by a chef in some stew;
He should have been told
That the gnu was too old,
For in stews only new gnus will do.

They bake some strange buns at Nuneaton
With dough that's first whipped and then beaten;
They have several tons
Of these fabulous buns,
But south of Nuneaton? None eaten!

A fisherman living in Deal,
When asked what he liked for a meal,
Said: "All kinds of fish,
But my favourite dish
Is a properly stuffed jellied eel."

CHARLES CONNELL

I sat next to the Duchess at tea.
It was just as I feared it would be:
Her rumblings abdominal
Were simply phenomenal,
And everyone thought it was *me!*

Think of those yummy fishfingers;
Think of the millions you eat –
Then think of the billions
And trillions and zillions
You'd swallow if fishes had feet!
ROGER WODDIS

There was a cantankerous 'gator
For whom 'twas no pleasure to cater;
If he happened to find
No dish on his mind,
He would like as not swallow the waiter!
OLIVER HERFORD

A haute cuisine author who sells
(Often lauded by literary swells),
Upon winning the Booker,
Purchased a new cooker
Which blew out and singed his quenelles!

Sardines seem to get out of hand
In a way I cannot understand;
For they never appear
At the table, I hear,
Unless they are tight, oiled, and canned.

There was an old drunkard of Devon
Who died and ascended to Heaven;
   But he cried: "This is Hades –
   There are no naughty ladies,
And the pubs are all shut by eleven!"
RON RUBIN

There's a cafe on t'far side of 'eath
That serves giant Yorkshire Puds with its beef;
   I kid you not mate –
   They're t'size of t'plate!
But they don't 'arf get stuck in yer teeth.

I'll start with the mulligatawny,
Then seafood, provided it's prawny;
   The lamb, no – instead
   I'll have the pig's head –
As long as it isn't too brawny.

A couple of boozers from Swaffham
Would seek out real ales, and then quaff 'em;
   The problem that made
   For the victualler's trade,
Was in getting the cost of 'em off 'em!

Well, if it's a sin to like Guinness,
Then that, I admit's, what my sin is;
I like it with fizz,
Or just as it is –
And it's much better for me than gin is!

When Veronica's mother made custard
She was clearly a little bit flustered;
Her daughter said: "What
You have got is too hot –
Put your specs on, the label says 'mustard'!"

As our scientists reach for the stars,
I am certain there's life upon Mars:
Those little green men
Gave the game away when
They exported their chocolate bars!

A seafood admirer called Sid
Ate a mountainous helping of squid;
But felt suddenly ill
When he looked at the bill –
The squid had cost three-hundred quid!

A greedy young fellow called Wrench
Owned a cat, two small dogs, and a tench;
One day, in a trice,
He cooked them with rice,
And called the dish something in French.

MICHAEL PALIN

An unfortunate chap from Bellevue
Got himself in a bit of a stew;
The carrots and meat
Got under his feet,
And the dumplings obscured his view.

The cannibal chieftain sat
Regarding his meal, pink and fat;
He turned to his cook,
With a quite worried look:
And said: " I'll not manage all *that*!"

I know a young chap who's much wiser
After failing the old breathalyser;
At the end of the year,
He'll be giving up beer,
In favour of fruit juice and Tizer!

A soldier, just new in the Reg,
Said: "There's something amiss with the veg!"
The Deputy Cook
Had misread the book,
And served the perimeter hedge!

"How much is your haddock with crumbs?"
"Just one moment while I do my sums –
  Now, just for the thrifty,
  This piece here is fifty,
And will fill small to middle-sized tums!"

A boy who ate too many peanuts,
Began to imagine he'd see nuts
  Wherever he looked
  (Shelled, salted or cooked) –
Do you think he might possibly be nuts?

Miss Muffet's mum, growing suspicious,
Wondered: "Dear, was your dinner nutritious?"
  She replied: "Curds and whey?
  No, I left them today,
And ate a big spider – delicious!"
FRANK RICHARDS

In her den 'neath an African sky,
Said a leopardess, heaving a sigh,
To her hungry young leopards:
"We've run out of shepherds –
Tonight there'll be no Shepherd's Pie."

I made lots of butterscotch fudge,
And then, while this sugary sludge
Was still piping hot,
I demolished the lot –
And it's so weighed me down, I can't budge!

A young lady too fond of meringue
Let concerns for her figure go hang;
She consumed them in tons,
Along with cream buns,
Until she went off with a BANG!

VAL POHLER

A greedy lad wolfing some jelly
The same time as watching the telly,
Discovered (too late)
He was chewing the plate –
Now small chunks of it lie in his belly.

There are cannibals near Timbuktu
Who make such a mouth-watering stew;
But, when asked to reveal
What comprises this meal,
Answer: "Gravy, potatoes – and you!"

"What makes you think I'm feeling sick,
After only four pancakes?" asked Dick,
"Six iced buns and some chops,
And a few ginger pops –
I'm fine, where's the bathroom? And *quick*!"

FRANK RICHARDS

A greedy old gourmet from Sydney
Consumed a huge pie (steak and kidney),
And imbibed much wine (red),
Whereupon he fell dead,
Still he went very happily, didn't 'e!

A hungry old fellow named Gumble
Whose tummy emitted a rumble,
And rumbled again,
Was heard to explain:
"It's calling for blackcurrant crumble!"

At dinner (in mood quite unpleasant),
An old duffer bit into roast pheasant;
He shoved back his chair,
And left his teeth where
They grinned madly at everyone present!

A large, gluttonous gent heard a shout:
"Hoi! Stop your over-indulging, you lout!"
Who on earth could it be?
Then a voice said: "It's me –
I'm the thin man inside, let me OUT!"

A greengrocer told me, quite stroppily,
That customers don't choose veg properly:
"They just pile their trolleys
With carrots and caulis
And butternut squashes and broccoli!"

I work in a patisserie,
Which isn't such good news for me:
In all my tea breaks,
I try different cakes –
I shall have to lie down *aujourd'hui!*

There was an old wino called Dieter
Who gulped down fine wine by the litre;
They worked out his bill
(At a restaurant in Rhyl)
By fitting his mouth with a meter!

A chap in a pub said: "I think
There's a black hairy thing in my drink!"
Said the barmaid, quite cool:
"It's a false eyelash, fool –
It often comes off when I blink."

A learned young lady called Betty,
Devoured all the works of Rossetti;
The prose and the ballads
She ate with her salads,
The sonnets she scoffed with spaghetti.

As he finished his dainty first course:
"I could eat," said the diner, "A horse!"
And that's just what the waiter
Brought in a while later,
All covered in cranberry sauce!

There's a girl out in Ann Arbor, Mich.,
To meet whom I never would wich;
She'll eat up ice-cream
Till with colic she'll scream,
Then order another big dich!

There was an old man of Spithead,
Who opened the window and said:
"I see two Isles of Wight –
What a hell of a night!
Oh, my head! I feel dead! Where's my bed?"
FRANK RICHARDS

There was an old man of Peru
Who watched his wife making a stew;
He said: "It's too thin."
So she pushed him in,
Saying: "Nobody's thicker than you!"
FRANK RICHARDS

There was a young lady of Ulva
Who drunkenly said: "What a hulva
   Party ya mizd,
   Why, I gozzo pizd –
I saw more lil' people than Gulva!"
BILL GREENWELL

As the natives got ready to serve
A midget explorer named Merv:
"This meal will be brief,"
Said the Cannibal Chief,
"For this is, at best, an *hors d'oeuvre*."

If 'high' for superfluous fat you rate,
And wish without setbacks to maturate,
   Keep far from your gut a
   Mere soupçon of butter
And stick to the polyunsaturate.

There was an old fellow named Price
Who was terribly partial to mice,
Which he kept in a cage
Till their coming-of-age,
When he fried them and ate them with rice!

A gluttonous schoolboy called Nick
Consumed several meat pies and was sick;
Then he howled: "It's not fair,
Now I'm so full of air,
I need six double-beefburgers. Quick!"

There once was a fellow named Bysshe
Who served up a meal of fish;
It was utterly raw,
As his dinner-guest's saw
When the starter swam twice round the dish!

A fussy old feller from Hutton
Enjoyed beef a lot better than mutton;
When is wife said: "It's dearer!"
He'd pretend not to hear her
Contemplating his top waistcoat button.

There was a young lady of Jarrow
Whose mouth was exceedingly narrow;
Though times without number
She had chewed a cucumber,
She'd never quite managed a marrow.
WILKIE BARD

K is for kind little Katie
Who weighs near a hundred-and-eighty;
   She eats ten times a day,
   And the doctors all say
That's the reason she's growing so weighty.

Rotund Raymond would frequently say:
"I am, primarily, a gourmet;
   Though of food I am fond,
   I am *not* a gourmand –
I do know when to call it a day!"

A ravenous lady of Wycombe
Much loves to pick apples and lycombe;
   One day, after tea,
   She devoured eighty-three –
An acquaintance said: "You don't half pycombe!"

I adore the Italian Deli
Where I buy stuff to fill up my belly:
   Mascarpone, rigatoni,
   Cannelloni, macaroni,
And tricolore tagliatelle.

Green Limericks

When a neutron meets friendly uranium
They react, safely sealed in titanium;
    The power you don't mind,
    But the waste left behind
Could zap half the cells in your cranium.
EMMA SCHOFIELD

There were two little green men from Mars
Who studied our gases from cars;
    "A hole will arise,"
They said, "In the skies –
We're glad it's your world and not ours!"

KATHERINE HANDLEY

Is the beach still a nice place to play?
Do you fancy a swim in the bay?
    Then make sure you don't sink,
    Or you might have to drink
What you passed on the previous day.
L. F. MENAGE

The political colouring book
Has suddenly got a new look:
They're all awfully keen
To be seen to be green –
How simple, yet how *long* it took!
P. R. BOWRING

There was a young lady of Perth
Who regarded the Greens with much mirth;
    Then she heard of the hole
    In ozone, at the Pole,
And now she's a Friend of The Earth.
FRANK DUNSTAN

An organic young gardener from Sale
Collected his slugs in a pail;
    "I hate pesticide!
    It's immoral!" he cried,
Before drowning the buggers in ale.
DAVID MATHER

They are chopping the rainforest down
To make way for another new town;
    Creatures are crying,
    The plants are all dying –
Mother Nature looks on with a frown.

JENNIFER HOWLISTON

Too long has this Earth of ours been
A dispiriting, desolate scene;
    Please, let's not destroy it,
    But live to enjoy it
By switching all systems to Green!
ALAN CLARK

An army of activist greens,
Each with sensitive feelings it seems,
Are protesting the massacres
Of poor, innocent brassicas
And assorted legumes, peas and beans.

As aliens passed in their craft,
They saw a blue planet and laughed:
   "I think it's called Earth,
   Give it a wide berth –
It stinks, and its people are daft!"
TIM WAITS

Oh, why doesn't anyone mind?
Why are we so cruel and so blind
   To the state of the seas,
   And the fate of the trees?
How come we are labelled Mankind?

B. MYERS

"The Earth has been quite a success,"
Said God, "But I have to confess:
   The Creation of Man
   Rather buggered the plan,
For he makes such a terrible mess!"
PHILIP BIRD

One day when the petrol runs out,
And the last tiny drop leaves the spout,
   I'll go where I like
   On my trusty old bike,
Saying: "How nice with no traffic about!"

CHARLOTTE LEWIS

There was a young yuppie from Ware
Who sneered at the Greens with long hair;
   With his Porsche, on the road,
   He was like Mr Toad,
Till he choked on the lead in the air.
SUE APPLETON

Said the seal to the salmon and otters:
"Did God really design us as blotters
   To mop up the oil
   From the sea and the soil,
Spewed out by those corporate rotters?"

    W. R. CROUCH

A wildlife gardener named Reg
Grew a haven of meadow and hedge:
   The birds ate the bugs,
   And the frogs ate the slugs,
And Reg ate the organic veg.
C. A. JONES

In fifty years time I declare,
Because of this greenhouse affair,
We'll spend our vacations
At seaside locations
Like Bradford or Slough-Super-Mare!
J. FIELDING

There once lived a foolhardy race
In a faraway corner of Space;
   Blind to its worth,
   They poisoned their Earth
And all disappeared, without trace.

RON RUBIN

A man with a chemical spray
Came drenching the orchard today;
   The death of the bee
   Will sting you and me –
Speak up for the earth while you may.

P.R. BOWRING

Today we've achieved a finesse
In packaging goods to excess,
   Using mountains of plastic,
   Foam, nylon – fantastic –
Tomorrow we'll clean up the mess.

RUTH BLANDFORD

In a frame of mind far from serene,
The chameleon said: "It's quite obscene!
   The world's in a mess,
   And I feel so distressed
I've a good mind to go and turn green!"

NOEL FORD

Said the Devil, with terrible mirth:
"They've made a great mess of the Earth:
   They kept cashing in
   On original sin –
Now it's mine, for the little it's worth!"
JOYCE DUNBAR

What on Earth's to be done about France?
They'll eat anything *larger* than ants;
   if it moves, it must die
   And be put in a pie –
Will they alter their habits? No chance!

An alien studying Earth,
And considering if it was worth
   Organizing a trip
   Redirected his ship
With a flick of the switch to 'Wide Berth'!
REG LYNES

I went on the Net for a surf,
And found 'Enemies of the Earth' –
   Irresponsible sorts
   Who had sold their world short,
Having little regard for its worth.

Animal Limericks

There were three little owls in a wood,
Who sang hymns whenever they could;
    What the words were about,
    One could never make out,
But one felt it was doing them good.

       The odd thing about Cecil Rhodes
      Was his fondness for natterjack toads;
          He'd eat them alive,
        Sometimes three, four or five,
     Hence his need for enormous commodes.

I once had a fully trained moth
Who'd swim like a fish in Scotch Broth;
    To end his routine
    He'd fart "God Save The Queen".
Has anyone here got a cloth?

            An old bear at Baraboo Zoo
          Could always find something to do;
            When it bored him to go
              On a walk to and fro,
         He'd about turn and walk fro and to.

There was a young lady named Maggie
Whose pet dog was awfully shaggy;
The front end of him
Looked quite vicious and grim,
But the tail end was friendly and waggy.

A Geordie dog lover I've met,
Left her ailing dachshund at the vet
With a tear in her eye
And, no simple goodbye,
But the thoughtful "Auf Wiedersehen, Pet".
REG LYNES

Our cat watches ads on the telly
That show chunky meatballs in jelly;
   She wants only those,
   So she turns up her nose,
Till she gets what she wants in her belly.
REG LYNES

I've a small breed of dog called a Scottie,
Who's house-trained and sits on a potty;
   He gives a loud yap,
   The mischievous chap,
Then stands up and wipes his own bottie.

The thoughts of the rabbit re: sex
Are seldom, if ever, complex;
For a rabbit in need
Is a rabbit indeed,
And does just as one might expect.

A menagerie came to Cape Grace,
Where they loved the gorilla's grimace;
It surprised them to learn
That he owned the concern,
He was human, in spite of his face!

A German explorer named Schlichter
Had a crush on a boa constrictor;
When he lifted its tail,
Achtung! It was male!
The constrictor, not Schlichter, was victor.

A sea-serpent saw a big tanker,
Bit a hole in her side and then sank her;
It swallowed the crew
In a minute or two,
And then picked its teeth with the anchor.

If he carries on like this he'll have t'go.
Where's the modest little chap we used t'know?
He's been pulling snooty faces,
And displaying airs and graces
Since he were given title Best in t'Show!
REG LYNES

If Hercules jumps up and bites you,
If he rips off your trousers and fights you,
If he tears you apart,
Eats your liver and heart,
He's just demonstrating he likes you!

REG LYNES

We keep a Columbian gorilla
Who's three times the size of Godzilla;
    She eats like a horse,
    Not a real one, of course,
Still it takes several truckloads to filla!
REG LYNES

        There was a young curate of Kew
        Who sat a tomcat on a pew;
        He taught it to speak
        Alphabetical Greek,
        But it never got farther than μ.

A freshman from down in Laguna
Fell madly in love with a tuna;
    The affair, although comic,
    Was so economic,
He wished he'd have thought of it sooner!

I'm a wisp of a wasp with a worry,
I'm hiding somewhere in Surrey;
    I've just bit upon
    The fat situpon
Of the King – so I left in a hurry!
COLIN WEST

A duck whom I happened to hear
Was complaining quite sadly: "Oh, dear!
Our picnic's today,
But the weathermen say
That the skies will be sunny and clear."

A sightseer from McAboo,
Observed a strange beast at the Zoo;
When she asked: "Is it old?"
She was smilingly told:
"It's not an old beast, but a gnu!"

Said an old racehorse owner named Groat,
Who owned a sleek racehorse of note;
    "I consider it smart
    To dine *à la carte*,
But my horse always takes *table d'oat*."

They tell of a hunter named Shepherd
Who was eaten for lunch by a leopard;
    Said the leopard: "Egad!
    You'd be tastier, lad,
Just a smidgen more salted and peppered!"

A nannygoat (hungry) called Heather,
Was tied up with a length of old leather;
In a minute or two
She had chomped it right through,
And that was the end of her tether.

The Hoover, in grim silence, sat,
But sucking no more at the mat;
    Quietly it grunted
    As slowly it shunted,
And messily disgorged the cat.
DAVID WOODSFORD

A French Poodle espied, in the hall,
A pool that a damp gamp let fall,
And said: "Ah, *oui, oui*!
This time it's not me,
But I'm bound to be blamed for it all."

There was a young lady of Ryde
Who was carried too far by the tide;
Cried a man-eating shark:
"How is this for a lark!
I knew that the Lord would provide."

A retired Civil Servant from Gateley,
Who lived in a home known as Stately,
Kept lions, for fun,
In a wire-netting run,
But he hasn't been seen around lately.

IDA THURTLE

Said an ape as he swung by his tail,
To his children both female and male:
"From your offspring, my dears,
In a couple of years,
May evolve a professor at Yale!"

A very young girl (call her Emma)
Was seized with a terrible tremma:
　　She'd swallowed a spider
　　Which spun webs inside her –
Good Lord! What an awful dilemma!

A farmer's one milking-cow, Zephyr,
Appeared such an amiable heifer;
　　Till one day, oh dear,
　　She kicked his right ear,
Which left him considerably deafer!

If you wish to descend from a camel
(That oddly superior mammal),
　　You simply must jump
　　From the hump on his rump –
He won't just pull up like a tram'll.

There was a young charmer named Sheba
Whose pet was a darling amoeba;
　　This odd blob of jelly
　　Would recline on her belly,
And dreamily murmur: *"Ich liebe."*

Said a miserly peer at the Abbey:
"I fear I shall look rather shabby,
For I've replaced my ermine
(infested with vermin),
With the fur of my dear defunct tabby."

Consider the poor hippopotamus:
His life is unduly monotonous;
He lives, half asleep,
At the edge of the deep,
And his face is as big as his bottom is.

An uncomfortable walrus named Stu
Who lived in a pool in the Zoo,
Once said to a friend:
"Do these teeth ever end?
I cannot see beyond them – can you?"

A lodger named Roger McBriggs,
Is having to find bigger digs,
For his pet cockatoo,
Anaconda, emu,
And a number of pot-bellied pigs!
REG LYNES

Said a rooster: "I want you to know
I am really the star of the show;
   The sun, that young pup,
   Would never get up
Unless I'd decided to crow!"

              There was a young lady from Burr
              Whose kitten had lovely soft fur;
                 She just loved to stroke it,
                 And pat it and poke it,
              For the pleasure of hearing it purr.

Jerome was a silly giraffe
Who wore a disguise for a laugh;
   Either he was too tall,
   Or the costume too small –
Did it cover Jerome? Only half!

              Said a crow to a pelican: "Grant
              Me the loan of your bill for my aunt;
                 She has asked me to tea."
                 Said the other: "Not me –
              Ask my brother, for this peli can't!"

Said two hunters: "Wild beasts? We don't mind them;
For we'll shoot them as soon as we find them."
    But while they (Fred and Ned)
    Stood and peered up ahead,
Sixteen elephants crept up behind them…

There once was a sailor named Link
Whose mates rushed him off to the clink;
Said he: "I've a skunk
As a pet in my bunk –
That's no reason to kick up a stink!"

At the Zoo I remarked to an emu:
"I just cannot pretend I esteem you –
    You're a greedy old bird,
    And your walk is absurd,
And not even your feathers redeem you."

There was an old bulldog named Caesar
Who went for a cat just to tease her;
    But she spat and she spit
    Till the old bulldog quit –
Now when poor Caesar sees her he flees her.

A monster who lived in a loch
Said: "I've suffered a terrible shoch;
    Some folk by the lake,
    Have called me a fake –
And my self-esteem's taken a knoch!"

A well-educated gorilla
Sat earnestly reading a thriller;
    "You cheat!" said his friend,
    "You peeped at the end –
So you know from the start who's the killer."

A cat with a great sense of fun
Stuck a bomb up a sleeping dog's bum;
To round off his caper,
He's lighted a taper,
And touched the blue paper – and run!

REG LYNES

A careless zookeeper named Blake
Fell into the tropical lake;
Said a fat alligator,
A few minutes later:
"Mmm, nice – but I much prefer steak."

A hippo from Chesapeake Bay
Decided to take up ballet:
She announced: "Well, here goes!"
Stood on tippy-toes,
And made a huge splash on Broadway.

Asked young fossil hunter, McBrumble:
"Did dinosaurs rattle and rumble?
Did they bellow, I wonder,
In voices like thunder,
Or merely just mutter and mumble?"

An elephant lay in his bunk,
In slumber his chest rose and sunk;
    He snored and he snored
    Till the jungle folk roared,
And his wife tied a knot in his trunk.

There was a young crab who said: "Fate
Has decreed I walk sideways, not straight;
    Oh, the bother and fuss
    When I run for a bus –
It's no wonder I'm so often late!"

In Summer the weather is hotter,
And out comes the butterfly spotter;
    The wasps and the bees
    Flit about 'neath the trees,
Till I squash them all flat with my swatter!

A puppy whose hair was so flowing,
There really was no way of knowing
    Which end was its head,
    Once stopped me and said:
"Please, sir, am I coming or going?"

You will find by the banks of the Nile
The haunt of the great crocodile;
 He will welcome you in
 With an innocent grin,
Which gives way to a satisfied smile.

You'd require an extremely long scarf
If you happened to be a giraffe;
 They get very hoarse
 In the Winter, of course,
And a sore throat's no reason to laugh.

Our parrot once let out a shriek
So that no one could hear themselves speak;
 But now we can hear,
 Since a bright engineer
Fixed a volume control to its beak.

A bull-voiced young fellow of Pawling
Competes in the meets for hog-calling;
 The people applaud,
 And the judges are awed,
But the hogs find it simply appalling!
MORRIS BISHOP

There once was an orang-utang
Who ate nothing else but meringue;
He sat on the floor
And consumed twenty four,
Till the greedy old monkey went bang!

The hedgehog said: "I'm feeling sickly –
Oh, why does my skin feel so prickly?"
    His girl said: "Hard lines,
    It's only your spines."
And she stroked them, but drew back quite quickly.

A Turk named Abdullah Ben Barum
Had sixty-five wives in his harem;
When his favourite horse died,
"Mighty Allah!" he cried,
"Take a few of my wives, I can spare 'em!"

There was a strange man in Dunluce,
Who would never say "Boo!" to a goose,
    Yet always said "Pooh-pooh!"
    On meeting a hoopoe,
And "Moo!" on observing a moose.

A certain dyspeptic old toucan
Said: "People think birds at the zoo can
Swallow any old thing,
From potatoes to string,
But if *I* can't, I'd like to know who can!"

If angered unduly, the curlew,
A look of defiance will hurl you,
As much as to say:
"Now, if I had my way,
I'd teach you, you impudent girl, you!"

A smart Aussie dingo called Rover
Whilst munching a strawberry pavlova,
Thought: "This is Down Under,
So, where then, I wonder,
Is that marvellous place called Up Over?"

A curious bird is the pelican:
His bill can hold more than his belican;
He can store in his beak
Enough food for a week,
But I'm blowed if I know how the helican!

As pets locusts aren't quite the ticket.
Tell the truth now, if asked would you pick it?
It would hardly enhance
Your expensive houseplants,
And, besides which, it just isn't cricket!

There was a young man from Tibet
With a fairly unusual pet;
    When his yeti fell sick,
    He was forced to think quick –
Should he summon the doctor, or vet?

The Pet Shop said *she* was a *he*!
So we went home, my rabbit and me;
    But it isn't so funny:
    Instead of one bunny,
I now have a hundred and three!

My delicate Siamese cat
Came home with a sizeable rat;
    She tossed it about,
    Turned it inside and out,
And left it for me on the mat.

Jack Russell, out walking one night,
Met old Boxer who wanted a fight;
They scrapped on the heath,
Jack lost several teeth,
Now his bark is much worse than his bite!

It's clear Peter Rabbit's a rotter:
Whenever the weather gets hotter,
Wherever he goes,
He's after the does,
Which doesn't impress Beatrix Potter!

Some chimpanzees sat in the Zoo
As the visitors passed, peering through;
When they gazed at each other,
It was hard to discover
Just who was examining who!

As Noah looked out with a frown,
He said:-"Crikey! It's chucking it down!
I'll knock up a boat
For the pets that won't float,
But at least the giraffes shouldn't drown!"

A camel with nothing to do
Thought he'd travel to Regent's Park Zoo;
   At the first intersection,
   He lost his direction –
And where is he now? Timbuctoo!

The Natterjack toad learned to knit
(Having nothing to wear that would fit);
   He knitted a jacket
   With buttoned-up placket –
The Natterjack's jacket's a hit!

MARY DANIELS

It is sad but it's true that the donkey
Can easily drive people wonky;
   For his musical skill
   Can be rated as nil,
Since he's more often off-key than on-key!

The donkey, a fat, lazy mule,
Will dig in his heels like a fool;
   But a sharp little prick,
   With the end of a stick
Does the trick, as a general rule!

There was an old chap with two poodles
Whose pet names were Toodles and Doodles;
    Their favourite dish
    Wasn't chicken or fish –
Those poodles loved oodles of noodles.

He muffets his way from the ceiling,
His long sticky bungee unreeling;
    And I, first unknowing,
    Quite bare, wet and glowing,
Scream loudly, my phobia revealing!

A dog with a bum for a head,
Who will answer to Freddy or Fred,
    Has no way of knowing
    If he's coming or going,
Or if he's still breathing, or dead!

An elderly bloodhound called Rix
Fancied juggling some balls and some sticks;
    He's had a good look
    In a Teach-Yourself book –
But you can't teach an old dog new tricks!

Two gruff grizzlies with not much to do,
Met a bear in the woods neither knew;
Well, imagine the roar,
When he offered his paw,
And said: "Hello. I'm Winnie The Pooh!"

An old Boxer Dog named McDuff
Runs away when the going gets tough;
He looks like he might
Punch his weight in a fight,
But the local cats think he's a puff!

A rodent, a bit of a rat,
Said: "But, darling, I can't afford that!"
And this tight-fisted mouse
Who won't spoil his spouse,
Adds: "It isn't the cost, it's the VAT!"

An overweight budgie named Billy
Decided to do something silly:
He broke out of his cage
(Quite a feat for his age),
And consumed fourteen pounds of Caerphilly!

A poodle, quite desperate to dance,
Said: "It's 'ruff' that one hasn't the chance
   To wow a Chihuahua,
   Or give a Chow Chow a
Fandango or Tango in France."

A venturesome three-week old chamois,
Strayed into the woods from his mamois;
   He might have been dead,
   But some picnickers fed
Him with sandwiches, milk and salamois.

It is the unfortunate habit
Of the rabbit to breed like a rabbit;
   One can say, without question,
   That this leads to congestion
In the burrows that rabbits inhabit.

"Please tell me," the chimpanzee said,
"Is it true what I've recently read?
Surely it cannot be
You're descended from me –
I thought monkeys were all so well bred!"
NOEL FORD

A polar bear grumbled: "I wish
I had something new in my dish,
Because grill it, or fry it,
Or boil it, my diet
Is fish, fish, fish, fish, fish and fish!"

NOEL FORD

An ostrich, prim, proper and pert,
Who buried her head in the dirt,
Was mistook, in the dark,
For a tree in the park,
And a passing dog gave her a squirt.

NOEL FORD

A promising, artistic weasel
Had erected his miniature easel;
But his country-lane scene
Turned out less than serene –
He was squashed by a twenty-tonne diesel!

NOEL FORD

I learned when attending nightschool:
Taxidermists have only one rule –
A creature must snuff it
Before you can stuff it
(The other way round would be cruel).

NOEL FORD

A flamingo I bought in a sale,
Has only one leg, long and frail;
I've been told by the vet,
If it breaks, not to fret –
There's a spare one tucked under its tail.

NOEL FORD

A chicken named Little once said:
"The sky's falling down on my head!"
A brainier bird
Might perhaps have referred
To our poor ozone layer instead.

NOEL FORD

A glow-worm once asked a close friend:
"Have you got a crash-helmet to lend?
There's a well-meaning lout
Who keeps stamping me out
In mistake for a cigarette-end!"

NOEL FORD

I once gave a thirsty giraffe
A coconut, just for a laugh;
I knew he would lack
The considerable knack
Of breaking it neatly in half.

COLIN WEST

Could you answer a small question, please:
Is it true that all mongrels have fleas,
    Whilst the Kennel Club types
    Have the best parasites,
With impeccable family trees?
NOEL FORD

If you're out shooting birds just for fun,
Here's something to reflect upon:
    Would you find it pleasant
    To meet a large pheasant,
If he was the one with the gun?
NOEL FORD

An elephant, known as Selina,
Was renowned for her helpful demeanour;
    But even *she* shrunk
    From allowing her trunk
To be used as a vacuum cleaner!
NOEL FORD

Stinging nettles are painful to some,
But not to the rhino, old chum;
    When I sit down, these prickles
    Are no more than tickles
To my armour-plate, bullet-proof bum!
NOEL FORD

A cow said: "I'm Friesian. You too?"
Her friend said: "I'm chilly, like you;
When we've finished our feed,
I know just what we'll need –
A couple of Jerseys will do!"

STAN STILL

An old Abyssinian monk
Was told by his colleagues he stunk;
It wasn't the rabbit
He hid in his habit,
But the skunk he kept under his bunk!

A miserable blackbird, quite surly,
Complained: "I am always up early,
But I never find bugs,
Caterpillars, or grubs,
And the earthworms I catch are too curly!"

I think we've been spotted from Venus:
Yes! A google-eyed alien has seen us;
It's massive, and red,
With huge horns on its head –
Three cheers for the space in between us!

A modest but talented duckling
Constructed a small clock, or clockling,
That went quack! when it struck,
Like an old daddy duck,
Which set all his duckling friends chuckling.

An elderly hound of Cohasset,
Introducing himself as a Basset,
Was told: "It's too bad
That your face looks so sad."
But replied: "My sad face is my asset!"

A sheikh, from the mountains of Riff,
Who returned from a journey, said: "If
Camels had wheels,
Like automobiles,
I would surely be feeling less stiff!"

An unfortunate farmer named Foster
Owned a prize-winning cow, but had lost her;
One fine afternoon,
There she was, in mid-June,
Scoffing grass in a garden in Gloster!

A painter at Coldwater Zoo
Was asked to touch up the old gnu;
Their leopard's black spots
Had faded to dots,
So he did a nice job on those too.

"Our tortoise has gone. Did you know?"
Said a lad to his mother, with woe;
 "How on earth can I tell?
 When I knocked on its shell,
And said 'Are you there?' it said "No!".

A poor little earthworm, they say,
Was chopped in two pieces one day,
By the merciless blade
Of a gardener's spade,
And the two of him wriggled away.

A bear who'd arrived at the Zoo,
When asked by a chimp: "Who are you?"
 Said: "My parents, for shame,
 Didn't give me a name –
So I'll be Rupert Paddington Pooh!"

An insect collector, displaying
His pets to a friend, was heard saying:
   "You may chat to the bees,
   And the ants, or the fleas,
But, please, not to the mantis – he's praying!"

Said a lonely old owl, full of gloom:
"Over field, town and village I zoom,
   But I don't get to know
   Any people below –
I may call out 'tu whit' but to whom?"

I've discovered a cure, quite dramatic,
That will keep my duck dry (she's rheumatic);
   A small bag of plastic,
   A band of elastic –
My aquatic pet is ecstatic!

An insect crawled onto a leaf,
Thinking: "I'll never lose my belief
In the big world outside,
So enormous and wide…"
Someone stamped on him. Isn't life brief?

A captive young eagle, from Spain,
Was dispatched on a journey by train;
    There's no point denying
    He'd much rather be flying,
So next time they'll send him by plane.

A lazy young puppy named Jinx
Thought: "It's funny how everyone thinks
    That all dogs delight in
    Much barking and fighting –
But me? I prefer forty winks!"

A fashionable tortoise named Price
Decorated his shell rather nice,
With silver and gold,
Maroon stripes (very bold),
And, on top, in bright yellow: KNOCK TWICE.

An animal lover named Cilla
Had saved up for a pet caterpillar;
    Her mother cried: "Stop!
    Take it back to the shop!"
So she did and brought home a gorilla!

As I understand it, the mink
Has no link with the skunk or the skink;
   A lizard's a skink,
   A skunk makes a stink,
And a mink's a large weasel – I think!
FRANK RICHARDS

"He's a curious fish is the flounder!"
Said the cod to the catfish, "The bounder!
   The rumour is rife
   That he murdered his wife –
The flounder. the bounder, he *drowned* her!"

Said a (distraught) young gardener named Pru,
Who'd just chopped a poor earthworm in two:
   "I know I'm to blame,
   But both ends look the same –
Which shall I apologise to?"

A famous white hunter from Tottenham
Rose up one fine day from his ottoman,
   And shot several llamas
   In his pink pyjamas –
"I wonder," he mused, "How they got in 'em?"
RON RUBIN

An affectionate barn owl flew
To a pretty young female he knew;
        But it started to rain,
        And he said, with disdain:
"I am leaving – it's too wet to woo!"

An animal breeder from Leigh
Had a dog that was strange as can be;
    When told: "But your hound
    Makes a loud ticking sound."
He explained: "It's a watch-dog d'you see!"
FRANK RICHARDS

A considerate cow (it was brown)
Saw the milkmaid was looking run down:
   "Don't worry, my dear,"
   The cow said, "Sit here,
And hang on while I jump up and down!"
PAUL ALEXANDER

A hyena once bet he could laugh
A lot louder than any giraffe;
   Hyenas please note:
   A giraffe has a throat
That produces a laugh and a half!

BILL GREENWELL

Said a young armadillo: "It's sad,
But I can't snuggle up to my dad,
   For an old armadillo
   Makes a very poor pillow,
Because of the way that he's clad.
PETER ALEXANDER

A dormouse, one dull autumn day,
Crawled in bed to sleep Winter away;
   But it didn't know
   The alarm clock was slow,
And awoke at a quarter past May!
FRANK RICHARDS

My friend, on a trip to the Zoo
Saw a parrot and shouted out "Coo!
Wot a bird! Wot a beak!
Can the 'orrid thing speak?"
Said the parrot: "Far better than you!"
FRANK RICHARDS

The vet said: "I'm going to need
Far more details before I proceed;
This form doesn't mention
Which leg needs attention."
The patient? A small centipede!
REG LYNES

A crab's eyes (the strangest I've seen)
Faced backwards on stalks coloured green;
It said: "Whilst not knowing
Which way I am going,
It helps to know where I've just been!"

A lion was rumbling inside.
His skeleton showed through his hide;
"I must bag a deer,
Or a decent sized steer –
I too, after all, have my pride."

A monkey exclaimed with great glee:
"The things in this Zoo that I see!
The curious features
Of all those strange creatures
That come and throw peanuts at me!"

FRANK RICHARDS

An elephant sat on some kegs,
And juggled glass bottles and eggs;
  And he said: "I surmise
  This occasions surprise –
But, oh dear, how it tires one's legs!"

A funny old lady named Borgia
Had a parrot whose nerve would have floored yer;
   Her mistress would whack her,
    And say: "Have a cracker!"
The bird would say: "Fire, nut, or Georgia?"

There was a young girl called Amanda
Who had a delightful pet panda;
She took it to school,
But it seems there's a rule
About pandas, and now they have banned her.*

*Not Amanda, the panda!

Said the boa to his wife; "Don't you find
That our bodies are poorly designed?
   Having spent half the day
   In constricting one's prey,
It is terribly hard to unwind!"

The hippo's an unlovely brute:
Huge, sluggish and irresolute;
   But don't smile so smugly –
   Though you think him ugly,
His momma, no doubt, thinks he's cute.

A naturalist of Beirut
Bought an owl, which turned out to be mute;
Said his wife: "How absurd
To have purchased a bird
That is mute, and does not give a hoot!"

"Those beasts at the Zoo," said young Gus,
"Are all so much bigger than us;
And the huge hippopotamus,
Well, he's got a bottom as
Big as the back of a bus!"

A handsome young noble of Spain
Met a lion one day in the rain;
He ran in a fright,
With all of his might,
But the lion, he ran with his mane!

There was an old man of the west
Who never could get any rest;
Some very large fleas
Used to meet on his knees,
Crawl up and play games on his chest.
FRANK RICHARDS

You may think that her boasting's a fag,
But a kangaroo's reason to brag;
    She never spends lots
    On push-chairs, or cots –
And just carries her babes in her bag.
FRANK RICHARDS

A man who deemed paper too dear,
Wrote a note on an elephant's ear;
    Said the postman: "At least
    Put a stamp on the beast,
And write Second-Class on its rear!"

A cow never thinks about mooing
Whenever she's occupied chewing;
    Processing the grass
    From the glade to the glass,
She must concentrate on what she's doing.
REG LYNES

A turkey who lived on a hill,
Awoke feeling really quite ill;
    "But why?" You may say.
    Well, it was Christmas Day –
A condition not cured by a pill!

A maggot decided to stop
With a girlfriend he'd met in a shop;
They married, post haste,
In a jar of meat paste,
And, much later, moved into a chop.

An extrovert, yodelling squirrel
Took a girlfriend to ski in the Tyrrol;
When she fell over twice,
She said: "This is not nice!"
And went home to her mum on the Wirral.

A diet-concious mountain gorilla
Tried his best to become somewhat slimmer;
He would go the whole day
On a mouthful of hay,
But then fill himself silly at dinner.

A centipede whose full name was Heather
Had a yen to wear shoes made of leather;
   This huge undertaking
   Has been long in the making,
And will probably go on forever.

A young fisherman landed a dace
That had whiskers all over its face;
   Said an onlooker: "That fish
   Is most surely a catfish.
For dace are clean-shaven, like plaice!"

An Antarctic penguin named Wayne,
Migrates every winter to Spain;
    But penguins can't fly,
    So he mutters "Goodbye",
And then catches the four-thirty train.

      A clever old chap from West Widgeon
      Once reared a talkative pigeon;
          He offered it bread,
          And it cawed and it said:
    "Oh, go on then – just give us a smidgeon!"

A wiry and sinuous eel
Fell in love with a plump lady seal;
    When he plighted his troth,
    She cried: "Get off you oaf!
Please, do me a favour – get real!"

An amoeba who lived in a pit,
Woke up one fine day, and said: "It
    Is time for vacation:
    I've found the location –
This year I am going to Split!"
RON RUBIN

A disgruntled old bear in a cage
Cried out in a terrible rage:
"There isn't much space,
And the food's a disgrace –
It's not healthy for someone my age!"

CHARLOTTE MCBEE

A curious beast is the lion:
His roar is no more than a try-on,
For his notion of fun
Is to lie in the sun –
How little a lion gets by on!

An animal lover named Jack
Wears wellies, false beard and a mac;
He wanders about
With his wife, who's a stout
Although not undesirable yak!

Sporty Limericks

The striker, a newly-signed star,
Had a chance but shot over the bar;
 His allegiance was tested
 When supporters suggested
The lad may have not had a pa!

In truth, in his youth, Babe Ruth
Could be a bit wild and uncouth;
But he became calmer,
With less melodrama,
When he grew more long in the tooth.
NICK TOCZEK

Ice Hockey is played at great speeds
By Canadians, Yanks, Finns, and Swedes;
 The aim of the game,
 It appears, is to maim –
A deployment that often succeeds.
RON RUBIN

A batter, named Fatty McPhatter,
Had the gift of the gab with his patter:
 "Whichever pitch comes,
 I hit only home runs –
So the fact that I'm fat doesn't matter!"

A wicked old scoundrel from Parker
Was renowned as a cunning card-sharper;
He'd swindle and cheat,
And then leap to his feet,
Make a grab for the winnings, and scarper!

They say that ex-President Taft,
When hit by a golf ball, just laughed,
And said: "I'm not sore,
But although he called 'Fore!',
The place where it struck me was aft!"

A golfer, employing a wedge,
Clipped his chip-shot behind a thick hedge;
But he hadn't been seen,
So he strolled to the green
And dropped a new ball on the edge.

If everyone else was much smaller,
Or you were a few inches taller,
You'd be the right size.
You're not. So, height-wise,
You're not quite a whole basketballer.

NICK TOCZEK

The Yankees were playing The Mets
On a million home TV sets:
"A team from New York
Will be walking the walk!"
Said an analyst (hedging his bets).

An overweight girl from Belfast
Took part in a race and came last;
As she ran out of puff,
Huffing: "I've had enough",
An old turtle came thundering past!

There's no-one so dreadful as Bender,
For batters whose bodies are tender;
He gets on their nerves
With his murderous swerves
That demand either death or surrender.

US Football, though played with élan,
Is a sport that we Brits love to pan,
'Cos that padded-out kit
Makes a guy look a bit
Too much like the Michelin Man!
RON RUBIN

Golf is a four-letter word
For a game that is clearly absurd;
Unless what you like
Is a long, boring hike,
Kitted out like a half-witted nerd!

RON RUBIN

An old guy from Wichita Falls
Went out and bought bats and some balls,
   Some gloves and kneepads –
   It's just one of his fads:
"Cos I never play Baseball!" he drawls.

There are three sorts of sailors: The Cruisers,
And The Racers (both winners and losers);
   And we all understand
   That, on reaching dry land,
The third kind appears – yes, The Boozers!

When we're covered in mud in the rain
Both our teams look exactly the same,
   And that last mucky maul
   Must have buried the ball –
Bugger it! Let's get on with the game!

A bowler could not hit the wicket,
And ran down in anger to kick it;
   As he sent the stumps flying
   And left the field crying,
The crowd shouted "Boo! *That's* not cricket!"

A poorly Man U fan I know,
Such a dedicated so-and-so,
Has been pronounced dead,
And the last thing he said?
"Here we go, here we go, here we go!"

A basketball player named Small,
Who was actually fourteen-foot tall,
Could score just by standing
And putting his hand in
The basket, and dropping the ball!

The slider just slid past the bat,
And the curveball? Too flat to get at;
The pitcher's last ball
Was his fastest fastball,
So I'm three-strikes-and-out. And that's that!

She had streaked around Lords and at Twickers,
Compromising a few dodgy tickers;
Her demise though was grisly,
When she tried it at Bisley –
If she'd only worn bullet-proof knickers!

Our captain exclaimed: "Holey-moley!
Look what's happened to our first-choice goalie."
      If his training routines
      Include eggs, chips and beans,
It's no wonder he's so roly-poly!"

CHARLOTTE MCBEE

A show-off whilst skating on ice,
Turned a difficult somersault (twice);
He bounced on his head,
Spat out six teeth and said:
"I must try that again – it was nice!"

I asked Santa Claus for some bed-socks
In the colours of (yep!) Boston Red Sox;
The next morning, there
Was the requisite pair
Of those hitherto-and-aforesaid socks!

I hit every home run we score;
I catch every catch and what's more
I ain't missed a game –
You may not know my name,
But I'm up here in row eighty-four.

When I was a full-back at Villa,
Our goalkeeper was a gorilla;
Athletic King Kong
Never put a foot wrong
In a seven-six, extra-time thriller!

Our keeper weighs four-hundred plus
In his protective clothing (and truss);
    And, if anyone charges,
    Or bullies, or barges,
He just flattens 'em – minimum fuss!

Basketball, a most interesting sport,
Is contested by teams on a court,
    With hooped nets and a ball;
    Though it helps if you're tall,
I'm afraid it's hard cheese if you're short!
RON RUBIN

This bloke's been at the crease since eleven,
For a boring grand total of seven;
    When the game is this slow,
    I would much rather go
For a holiday fortnight in Devon.

Though a pantomime horse ran so fast,
Premature celebrations were dashed;
    True, the head-end had won
    By a neck from Red Rum,
But the back-end pulled up at the last!
REG LYNES

The Irish competitor, sensing
Olympic Gold, felt himself tensing;
Was he likely to fail
With his best post and rail
In the opening round of the fencing?

REG LYNES

A lady who's not all that stunning,
Competes in much marathon running;
She really enjoys
Being chased by the boys –
Is she sporting, or simply quite cunning?

A powerful golfer named Lowndes
Hit his tee shot so far out of bounds,
He caught several planes,
Greyhound buses and trains,
Before he could finish his round.

The adventurous Percival Pope,
Had decided to ski down a slope;
But the slope was so steep,
And the snow was so deep –
Did our hero survive? I hope…nope!

A batsman from Sydney called Fairlie
Hit a very fast ball good and squarely;
A fielder called Reith
Caught the ball in his teeth –
A thing which he did very rarely.
MICHAEL PALIN

BIG LEE MERICK

A tower of strength in each game,
A powerful gigantic frame;
Mean, moody, colossal
Of menace and muscle,
A triumph of brawn over brain.
PAUL COOKSON

There was a plus-four of Wamsutter
Whose thoughts were too pungent to utter,
When his wife, as he found,
"Ere commencing a round,
Had been whisking the eggs with his putter!

An athletic young fellow called Mike
Went out for a ride on his bike;
He had such a bad fall
When he hit a brick wall,
He's decided, in future, he'll hike!

JOE SPALDING

A javelin thrower called Vicky
Found the grip of her javelin sticky;
    When it came to the throw,
    She just couldn't let go –
Making judging the distance quite tricky.

MICHAEL PALIN

Yelled a jockey at Monmouth Racecourse,
As he galloped with hurricane force:
"I've beaten the lot!"
But the crowd yelled: "You clot!
Go back. You've forgotten your horse!"

FRANK RICHARDS

To you Yanks, I have just this to say:
"American Cricket? No way!
    We pause when there's rain,
    But how we'd complain
If a sudden tornado stopped play!"

NICK TOCZEK

I bowled my best googlie at Gatting,
Who is fairly accomplished at batting;
Still he misjudged the flight
(It swerved left, then dipped right),
And he said something rude, but in Latin.

REG LYNES

A goalkeeper christened "The Cat"
Has been transferred for peanuts (plus VAT);
He acquired his name
In a vital Cup game –
He curled up in his box for a nap!

A golfer who hailed from Verdun
Was intent on not being outdone;
To avoid any glitches,
He carried spare britches,
In case he got a hole in one.

A wrestler said: "I'm in a spot!
The pace is becoming too hot;
My opponent's unfair –
He's pulled out my hair,
And tied both my legs in a knot!"

FRANK RICHARDS

A golfer tries hard to survive,
With grit, dedication and drive;
"Inflation," he'll claim
"Is affecting my game –
I used to shout 'fore', now it's 'five'."

There is a young golfer at Troon
Who always plays golf with a spoon;
"It's handy, you see,
For the brandy," says he,
"If some poor soul happens to swoon."

There once was a fellow called Grover
Who bowled seven wides in an over,
Which had never been done
By an Archdeacon's son
On a Tuesday, in August, at Dover!

The diagnosis of our first-team boss is:
The reason for our recent losses?
We're all in a dream,
We don't play like a team,
And our goalie is useless with crosses!

I played a few times for the Yankees
(Though, as memories, I've tried to blank these);
I did what I could,
But I wasn't much good,
And my antics had fans grabbing hankies.

A kick-boxer named Basher McBeer,
Stepping into the ring knew no fear;
Of fame he'd high hopes,
But instead the poor dope's
Ended up with a cauliflower rear!

A big-hitter, nicknamed The Slog,
Hit a fly ball and started to jog;
His homer (immense)
Flew right over the fence,
And landed in someone's hotdog!

A seven-stone weakling called Andy
Thought that weight-lifting might come in handy;
He practised the sport,
But was left quite distraught
When his poor little legs became bandy,

Said a Yank, who was over from Yonkers,
Whilst watching his first game of conkers:
"This game's a weird thing –
Just a nut on a string:
Now I know that you Brits are all bonkers!"

"Gosh, archery's fun!" gasped young Snape,
As he watched with his mouth all agape;
And when a stray shaft
Grazed his ear, he just laughed:
"Now I call that an arrow escape!"
RON RUBIN

A cricketing bowler called Patrick
Once scored a historical hat-trick;
What made the event
So bizarre, was the gent
Was a hundred. and quite geriatric.
RON RUBIN

A marathon runner from Cannes
Once ate fourteen kilos of bran;
His performance was stunning :
He couldn't stop running –
He just ran and he ran and he ran...
RON RUBIN

Now, Baseball is truly the ticket:
The game's so exciting and quick, it
Never gets boring;
Other sports have me snoring –
Like bowls, darts, golf, croquet and cricket...
RON RUBIN

Said a petite young housewife named Swales,
Who turns out in the back row for Wales:
"It's not normally done,
But, as well as great fun,
It's good prep for the end-of-year sales!"

A young mountaineer from Stock
Had climbed up a precipitous rock,
But she fell from the peak,
And, when able to speak,
Said: "That didn't half give me a shock!"

When I fell asleep we were winning,
At the start of our last-but-one inning;
   But when I awoke
   (All those beers and that coke!),
All the other supporters were grinning!

Don't tell me the score, please, I pray –
I shall watch it on Match of the Day;
   "You need worry no more,
   I won't tell you the score –
There weren't any goals anyway!"
REG LYNES

A courteous spin-bowler called Bubblebrew
Ventured: "Umpire, so sorry to trouble you;
   I've no wish to intrude,
   Or appear to be rude,
But – wasn't that out, lbw?
CHARLOTTE MCBEE

A team playing Baseball in Dallas
Called the umpire "blind" out of malice;
   While this worthy had fits,
   The team scored eight hits,
And a girl in the bleachers called Alice!

A batsman was struggling on nought,
When the umpire signalled: "Out, caught!"
His average was 'none'
From an eighteen-match run,
So he's thinking of changing his sport.
CHARLOTTE MCBEE

Grab your gun! Let's go hunting for fun!
I adore seeing beasts on the run!
There's nothing as pleasant
As blamming a pheasant –
It's so awfully exciting, *do* come!

A nimble young gymnast named Fritz
Did, as his finale, the splits;
It raised such a laugh
As he split right in half,
And was carried away in two bits!

A guy watching the game at Kaycee
Said to someone in front: "I can't see!"
"I'm an umpire, you crackpot!
You must take the jackpot
For having less sense than a flea!"

An ambitious young baseball player
Consulted a wise old soothsayer,
To be told: "You're OK,
Although not far away
Is the day you'll be playing okayer!"

NICK TOCZEK

I'm giving this next pitch a bunt
Just a couple of inches in front;
So the boys on each base
Will all move round one place –
It's a very unpopular stunt!

An inflexible hunter named Potter
Caused a clambering rambler to totter.
Explaining his reason,
He laughed: "It's the season –
And she claimed she was game, so I shot her!"

CHARLOTTE MCBEE

I was told that my football-mad chum
Had been so badly mauled in a scrum;
One poor ear, I hear,
Ended up in the beer,
And his teeth in a quarterback's bum!

Clever Limericks

There was a young man who said: "Damn!
It is borne in upon me I am
    An engine that moves
    In predestinate grooves,
I'm not even a bus, I'm a tram."
MAURICE HARE

There was a young lady called Wyatt
Whose voice grew incredibly quiet,
Until one day
It just faded away...

ON PROFESSOR COUE
This very remarkable man
Commends a most practical plan:
    You can do what you want
    If you don't think you can't,
So don't think you can't think you can.
CHARLES INGE

Animula vagula·blandula,
is it true that your origin's glandular?
must you twang for the Lord
an umbilical chord
like all other impropagandula?
CONRAD AIKEN
[Animula Vagula Blandula = little wandering gentle soul]

"If you're aristocratic," said Nietzsche,
"It's thumbs up, you're OK. Pleased to mietzsche.
If you're working-class bores,
It's thumbs down and up yours!
If you don't know your place, then I'll tietzsche."
GERRY HAMILL

Said an erudite sinologue: "How
Shall I try to describe to you Tao?
It is come, it is go,
It is yes, it is no,
Yet it's neither – you understand now?"
R. J. P. HEWISON

A sleeper from the Amazon
Put a nightie of his gramazon –
The reason was that
He was getting too fat
To get his own pajamazon!

There once was an African Mau-Mau
Who got into a terrible row-row;
The cause of the friction
Was his practising diction,
Saying: "How-how now-now brown-brown cow-cow."

A right-handed fellow named Wright,
In writing "write" always wrote "right"
Where he meant to write right;
If he'd written "write" right,
Wright would not have wrought rot writing "rite".

Said a boy to his teacher one day:
"Wright has not written 'rite' right, I say."
And the teacher replied,
As the error she eyed:
"Right! Wright, write 'write' right, right away!"

There was a young fellow of Beaulieu
Who loved a fair maiden most treaulieu;
He said: "Do be mine."
And she didn't decline,
So the wedding was solemnized deaulieu.

There was a young lady of Slough
Who went for a ride on a cough;
The brute pitched her off
When she started to coff –
She won't ride on such animals nough.
LANGFORD REED

A pretty young teacher named Beauchamp
Said: "These awful boys, how shall I teauchamp?
For they will not behave
Although I look grave,
And, with tears in my eyes, I beseauchamp."

A man, seeking moral direction,
In a mirror sought self-introspection;
He got quite a shock
As he sadly took stock –
He was worse than he thought, on reflection.

A card-playing lady named Sheila
Once 'led out' the King as a feila;
    When she saw her *faux pas*
    (For it didn't gaux fas),
She stuck out her tongue at the deila!

A fellow who lisped went to Merthyr
To woo a young maiden named Berthyr;
    He asked: "Have you been kitht?"
    But when she said: "Dethitht!"
He murmured: "She's let me down. Curthyr!"

There was a young lady named Wemyss
Who, it seems, was much troubled with dremyss;
    She would wake in the night
    And, in terrible fright,
Shake the bemyss of the house with her scremyss.

A tutor who taught on the flute
Tried to teach two young tooters to toot;
    Said the two to the tutor:
    "Is it harder to toot, or
To tutor two tooters to toot?"

A canny Scotch lad of Pitlochry
Kissed an up-to-date girl in a rochry;
When he tasted the paint,
He cried: "Lassie, this ain't
A real kiss at all, it's a mochry!"
LANGFORD REED

There was a mechalnwick of Alnwick,
Whose opinions were anti-Germalnwick;
So when war had begun
He went off with a gun,
The proportions of which were Titalnwick!

There was a young man of Cadiz
Who inferred that life is what it is;
For he clearly had learnt
If it were what it weren't,
It could not be that which it is.
J. ST LOE STRACHEY

In New Orleans dwelt a young Creole
Who, when asked if her hair was all reole,
Replied with a shrug:
"Just give it a tug,
And decide by the way that I squeole."
ALBEN BARKLEY

Said a pupil of Einstein: "It's rotten
To find I'd completely forgotten
    That by living so fast,
    All my future's my past,
And I'm buried before I'm begotten."
C. F. BEST

An early psychologist, Freud,
Had the bluenoses very anneud;
    Saying: "You cannot be rid
    Of the troublesome id,
So it might just as well be enjeud!"

A certain young chap named Bill Beebee
Was in love with a lady named Phoebe;
    "But," he said, "I must see
    What the clerical fee
Be before Phoebe be Phoebe Beebee."

A merchant, addressing a debtor,
Set down in the course of his lebtor:
    "I choose to suppose
    A man owes what he owes,
And the sooner he pays it, the betor!"

A gent with a drooping moustache
Chewed some hair, by mistake, eating hash;
   The phrases profane
   That he shrieked in his pain
We shall represent here with a – (dash)

My typist's undoubtable glamour
Didn't quite compensate for her gramour;
   She got me so ired,
   That I told her: "You're fired!"
But I wish she was back again, damour!

      A canner, exceedingly canny,
    One morning remarked to his granny:
        "A canner can can
        Anything that he can,
   But a canner can't can a can, can he?"
                CAROLYN WELLS

A lass who weighed many an oz
Used expressions nice girls don't pronoz,
   When a prankster, unkind,
   Yanked her chair from behind
Just to see, he explained, if she'd boz.

The Honorable Winifred Wemyss
Saw styli and snakes in her dremyss;
    And these she enjeud,
    Until she heard Freud
Utter: "Nothing is quite what it semyss!"

A bright little lassie in Lawrence
Used language that came out in tawrence;
    Till, informed by her teacher:
    "Your manners, dear creacher,
Are worse than your scholarship wawrence."

There was an old lawyer named Dolan
Whose income was happily swollen
    By charging huge fees
    For interpreting these:
    The , the – and the :
    [The comma, the dash and the colon.]

There was a young lady from Delaware
Who was most undoubtedly welaware
    That to dress for a masque
    Wasn't much of a task,
But she cried: "What the hell will my felaware?"

Endeavoured a lady of North Dak
To picture a bear with a Kodak;
The button was pressed,
The bear did the rest –
She didn't stop running till South Dak.
[NB North Dak is an abbreviation of North Dakota]

A lad who dyed cotton in Lancashire
Was always engaging in Prancashire;
One day, sad to say,
He tripped in his play,
And sank in his own dyeing tancashire.

A philosopher Fellow of Trinity
Said: "Geometry shows this affinity:
Concavo-convex is
Symbolic of sexes,
While arrows denote masculinity."

If no Pain were, how judge we of pleasure?
If no work, where's the solace of Leisure?
What's White, if no Black?
What's Wealth, if no Lack?
If no Loss, how our Gain could we measure?
WILLIAM BLISS

A lady from Atlanta, Ga,
Became quite a notable fa;
    But she faded from view
    With a quaint IOU
That she signed: "Mrs Lucrezia Ba".
[NB Ga is an abbreviation of Georgia]

She had pouted and shouted: "Oh, Mr!"
Because in the swing he had ks;
    And so, for sheer spite,
    Later on that same night,
This Mr had ks young sr.

        There was an old dame of Dunbar
        Who took the 4.4 to Forfar;
        But went on to Dundee,
        So she travelled, you see,
        Too far by 4.4 from Forfar.

Two maidens were seated at t,
Discussing the things that might b;
    "I think I'll wed Willy,"
    Said Molly to Milly,
"That is, if he asks me, you c."

There was a young man named Colquhoun
Who kept, as a pet, a babuhoun;
His mother said: "Cholmondley,
I don't think it colmondley
That you feed your baboon with a spuhoun!"

Said a greedyguts youngster named Beauchamp:
"Those jelly tarts, how shall I reauchamp?
   To my parents I'd go,
   But they'd only say no,
No matter how much I beseauchamp!"

A young Irish servant in Drogheda
Had a mistress who often annogheda,
   Till she finally swore
   In a language so raw
That thereafter nobody emplogheda!

A Bolshevik, living in Bedfordshire,
Said: "I'll see, when my only son wedfordshire,
   His bride's not in white,
   Like a pre-Raphaelite,
But robed in the reddest of redfordshire!"

There was an old lady of Weasenham
Whose bedclothes had too many fleas in 'em;
   So she covered the sheeting
   With masses of Keating,
Which made all the fleas in 'em sneeze in 'em.

A ghost from a graveyard in Havant
Discussed world affairs with a savant;
   But when asked to abjure
   Being quite so obscure,
Said: "I thought I was being transparent!"

In trying to rhyme the word "orange",
Couldn't "porringer" contract to "porringe"?
And, as compensation,
Allow the Scots nation
Expansion of "sporran" to "sporrange"!

The great violinist was bowing.
The quarrelsome oarsmen were rowing;
   But how is the sage
   To judge from the page:
Was it piglets or seeds that were sowing?

Said a logical linguist named Rolles:
"As we always call Polish folk Poles,
For better precision
(I am a logician),
We ought to call Dutch people Holes."

It is time to make love, douse the glim.
The evening sky becomes dim.
  The stars will soon peep,
  As the birds fall asleep,
And the loin shall lie down with the limb.

Someday ere she grows too antique,
My girl's hand in marriage I'll sicque;
  If she's not a coquette
  (Which I'll greatly regret),
She shall share my ten dollars a wique.

There was an old man in a boat
Who said: "I'm afloat! I'm afloat!
  I speak when I talk;
  I move when I walk –
That's logic!" The silly, old goat.
FRANK RICHARDS

I suppose I could try if I chose,
But the question is: "Can I suppose
  I could *choose* what I chose if
  I chose?" I suppose if
I chose to. But nobody knows.

A Cynic says: "Now that we know
Life's a futile, incessant flow,
And there's really no knowing
The way it is going,
I am going to let myself go!"
THOMAS THORNELEY

The truth about truth is elusive;
Is philosophy merely delusive?
What seems rubbish to you
May be for me true,
Which leaves everything inconclusive.
E. O. PARROTT

There once was a man of Madrid
Whose ego was swamped by his id;
The subsequent trauma
Extinguished the former,
While the latter just murmured: "Well rid!"

There was a faith-healer of Deal
Who said: "Although pain isn't real,
   If I sit on a pin,
   And it punctures my skin,
I dislike what I fancy I feel."

Silly Limericks

The Barbarian, Morgan the Mighty,
Is suspected of being quite flighty;
    A six-foot-eight hulk,
    His considerable bulk
Does look cute in a winceyette nightie!

The funniest man that I've met
Keeps a very large rock as a pet;
    It's as quiet as a mouse,
    Makes no mess in the house,
And he never pays bills to the vet.

FRANK RICHARDS

A sprightly Norwegian, named Bjork,
Popped out for an afternoon walk;
    We knew he walked fast,
    But that night were aghast
When he called to say "Hi!" from New York!

CHARLOTTE MCBEE

A man who counts woodlice, named Dunne,
Has counted eight billion and one;
He lays on the ground
Where the woodlice abound,
And insists counting woodlice is fun.

There was a young girl from Peru
Who cried: "Yes, I do! Yes, I do!"
When asked what she did,
She ran off and hid –
We don't know where she's hiding, do you?

A handyman felt moved to boast:
"Repairing is what I like most."
Now his cooker can play
Lively music all day,
While his radio burns all the toast!

FRANK RICHARDS

I once spent a weekend in Hove
With a most unattractive old cove;
He said proudly: "I am
The great Jean Claude Van Damme!"
But he wasn't – his y-fronts were mauve.

A long-distance driver named Wally
Apprehended by police said: "I'm sorry,
You've got the wrong man,
What, me? Nicked this van?
Nah – it fell off the back of a lorry!"
REG LYNES

A little known fact about Plato:
He invented the concept of NATO,
The Swiss Army Knife,
The Inflatable Wife,
And the Trouserless Jacket Potato.

While leafing my way through *The Times*,
I read the bizarrest of crimes.
It appears, in Rangoon,
A man sued a baboon.
Not funny, but be fair, it rhymes.

There was an old person of Fratton
Who would go to church with his hat on;
"When I wake up," he said,
"With my hat on my head,
I shall know that it hasn't been sat on."

A gardener (quite mad) from the Borders,
Puts a mixture of things in his borders:
   Such as the Principal (fool!),
   Several day boys from school,
And a couple of bothersome boarders!

The record for eating black pudding
Belongs to a chap called Jack Gooding;
   The poor gentleman died
   When he opened up wide,
And shoved all the pudding he could in.

REG LYNES

Chocoholic, the great General Custer
Cried, with typically soldierly bluster:
   "Sitting Bull's out of luck –
   He's become Sitting Duck,
After stealing that last nutty cluster!"

A forgetful old fool called O'Reilly,
Keeps insisting his name is O'Really;
   On the evidence, clearly,
   He knows his name (nearly) –
"I'm O'Really!" O'Reilly says wryly.

An Eskimo from the North Pole
Has learned to speak English, I'm told;
The one useful phrase
Which he uses most days
Is: "Don't ask if I'm feeling the cold."

A skeleton once, in Khartoum,
Invited a ghost to his room;
They spent the whole night
In the eeriest fight
As to who should be frightened of whom.

A deep-water sailor called Rod
Used to dive in and rescue live cod;
He wasn't a fool
Who thought it was cruel,
But he certainly was pretty odd.
MICHAEL PALIN

There was a young girl in the choir
Whose voice arose higher and higher;
Till one Sunday night
It rose out of sight,
And was found the next day on the spire.

He died in attempting to swallow,
Which proves that, though fat, he was hollow;
For in gasping for space
He swallowed his face
And hadn't the courage to follow.

A fellow of little renown
Is becoming the talk of the town;
His most recent quirk is
To think he's a circus,
When really he's only a clown.

At the party they've started a conga,
And the Indian File's getting longer,
And longer and longer
And longer and longer
And longer and longer and longer…

A young mountaineer called Vic
Became quite close friends with a stick;
He took it for walks,
And they had little talks,
Then it left him to live with a brick.

MICHAEL PALIN

There once was a boy of Bagdad,
An inquisitive sort of a lad;
He said: "Let us see
If a sting has a bee."
And quickly found out that it had.

There was an old man who said: "Do
Tell me how does one add two and two?
I'm not very sure
That it doesn't make more,
But I fear that is almost too few!"

There was an old man of Boolong
Who frightened wild birds with his song;
    It wasn't the words
    That astonished the birds,
But the horrible *dooble ontong!*

The man who invented the sprocket,
Went on to develop the socket;
Then one afternoon,
He shot to the moon –
That's right! He'd invented the rocket!

There was a young man of Dumfries
Who had the most knobbly knees;
If he went to the park,
He would go after dark,
For dogs often mistook him for trees!

A bear who will eat only honey
(Preferring the thick to the runny),
    Has been bitten by bees
    On all four of his knees,
Which he found not one little bit funny.

A curious bird is the crow,
Quite the blackest of fowl that I know;
    Though it's well out of sight
    In the deep of the night,
How on earth does it hide in the snow?

A kindly old fellow called Clore
Gave all that he had to the poor;
    But, alas and alack,
    They would not give it back,
So he's not giving them anymore.

MICHAEL PALIN

A very light sleeper called Lowndes
Would wake at the slightest of sounds,
    Like a fish thinking hard,
    Or the rustling of lard,
Or moles far beneath football grounds.

MICHAEL PALIN

There was a young girl from Asturias
Whose temper could often be furious;
   She hurled boiled eggs
   At her grandmother's legs –
A habit unpleasant yet curious.

When asked tricky questions, old Riley
Would simply reply, very dryly:
"I'm sorry, old bean,
I don't know what you mean."
Then sidle off home, smiling wryly.

MICHAEL PALIN

A man on a length of elastic,
Decided to do something drastic;
   When he jumped off the cliff he
   Came back in a jiffy,
And screamed to his friends: "It's fantastic!"
MICHAEL PALIN

There was an old chap from Fort Wayne
Who couldn't remember his name;
"I'm Willy McBread!"
"You're silly," they said,
"Better hurry, or you'll miss your train!"

CHARLOTTE MCBEE

There was a young lady of Venice
Who used hard-boiled eggs to play tennis;
When they said: "It seems wrong."
She remarked: "Go along!
You don't know how prolific my hen is!"

There was a young man from Lorraine
Who was hoisted aloft by a crane;
His screams went unheard,
Except by a bird
That was busy migrating to Spain.

They asked Edward Moppet of Leeke
(Whose conception of time was quite bleak):
"How often, dear Ted,
Do you bath?" And he said:
"Once on Saturday night, twice a week!"

An Australian native, one day,
Bought a new boomerang with his pay;
But he broke down and cried,
For, however he tried,
He could not throw the old one away!

A fellow named Phineas Fly
Resides in a muddy pigsty;
If you asked why this was,
He'd reply: "Oh, because
It is none of your business, that's why!"

A gravedigger's helper called Maddox
Was obsessed with an urge to ride haddocks;
He made little paddles,
And waterproof saddles,
But the fish never stayed in the paddocks.

MICHAEL PALIN

A boy, treasure hunting, went down
To the big rubbish tip outside town;
    There were bedsteads and cars,
    And old pickle jars,
And the Royal Albert Hall, upside down!

There was a young lady named Joyce
Who said: "I've no r's in my voice;
    But I dance wock and woll,
    Wear a wabbit-skin stole,
And dwive in a swanky Woll's Woyce!"

Plutonious Puffington Brown,
A much recognized man-about-town,
    Said: "This name of mine's length,
    Quite wears out my strength,
And it takes *such* an age to write down!"

A Lollipop Lady from Poole,
One day felt like playing the fool;
    And that's what she did:
    She stopped every kid,
And sent fifteen lorries to school!

There was a young lady of Wheeling
Who had the peculiar feeling
That she was a fly,
And wanted to try
To walk upside down on the ceiling.

A fellow from Boston named Lance
Couldn't walk well or run well, or dance;
It troubled his mind
Till he happened to find
That his necktie was caught in his pants.

If all the world were paper,
And all the sea were ink,
And all the trees
Were bread and cheese,
What would we do for drink?

There was a young girl who asked: "Why
Can't I look in my ear with my eye?
If I put my mind to it,
I'm sure I can do it –
You never can tell till you try!"

There was an old lady who said,
When she found a thief under her bed:
"So near to the floor,
And so close to the door –
I'm afraid you'll catch cold in your head!"

A silly young fellow named Ted
Walks around with a cat on his head;
When asked why a cat
Instead of a hat,
"Well, a horse is too heavy!" he said.

There was an old wizard of Rhodes
Who wrote lots of sonnets and odes;
His wife was a witch,
And they lived in a ditch
On a diet of lizards and toads.

There was an old Man in the Moon
Who came down to Earth by balloon;
Said Father: "If he's
Really made out of cheese,
Will somebody fetch me a spoon!"

There was a young boy in a tree
Who was horribly stung by a bee;
I won't tell you where
(It wouldn't be fair),
But he always stands up for his tea!
FRANK RICHARDS

A very odd fellow called Ned
Had eyes in the back of his head;
There was no way of knowing
Which way he was going,
"But I know where I've been to!" he said.

A circus ring-master named Mike
Went fishing and landed a pike;
In a matter of weeks
It was juggling leeks,
And riding a wobbly bike!

A peculiar fellow named Sam
Developed a thing about ham;
He'd purchase a shoulder
The size of a boulder,
And push it around in a pram!

Arty Limericks

"Having children," said Evelyn Waugh,
"Is really a bit of a bore;
We wanted a few,
But when Auberon was two,
We said: 'Oh, let's not have any more'."

There's a lady who reads Mills & Boon
By the light of the silvery moon;
She loves all the stories,
And votes for the Tories,
They'll be coming to get her quite soon.

A book and a jug and a dame,
With a nice cosy nook for the same;
"And I don't give a damn,"
Uttered Omar Khayyam,
"What you say, it's a great little game!"

A Kentucky-based author named Vaughan
Whose style often savoured of scorn,
Soon inscribed in his journals:
"Here the corn's full of kernels,
And the colonels are all full of corn."

A sculptor remarked: "I'm afraid
I have fallen in love with my trade;
I am much too elated
With what I've created –
That's mainly the women I've made."

This production of *Lear* is a frolic:
They've made the old man melancholic,
Climbing up all the trees,
Swinging from the trapeze,
And juggling with plates – how symbolic!

FRANK RICHARDS

I once spent a weekend in Brighton
With the legendary Miss Enid Blyton;
She said: " You be Noddy,
And I'll show you my body,"
But Big Ears kept turning the light on.

There was a great German grammarian,
Whose grandmother wasn't an Aryan;
So his books have been burned,
And his person interned,
And his doctrine denounced as barbarian.

Shelley's death – was it really his wish
To be drowned 'midst Italian fish?
I certainly think
I'd dive in the drink
If my parents had christened me Bysshe.

BILL GREENWELL

Our novels get longa and longa.
Their language gets stronga and stronga;
There's much to be said
For a life that is led
In illiterate places like Bonga.

H. G. WELLS

The wife of the bard, Geoffrey Chaucer,
Said: "Don't sip your tea from your saucer
Your Tales, I suspect,
Have an adverse effect –
They are making you coarser and coarser."
FRANK RICHARDS

Said an ardent booklover in Siam:
"I frequently read Omar Khayyam;
His morals depress me,
But nevertheless he
Is almost as clever as I am!"

There was a young man of Moose Jaw
Who wanted to meet Bernard Shaw;
When asked as to why,
He made no reply,
But sharpened his circular saw.

A literary person name Hilton,
When he read Robert Burns, put a kilt on;
He dressed in a cope
Whilst reading from Pope,
And a nightshirt if studying Milton.

SIR JOSHUA REYNOLDS (1723–1792)

A painter of portraits, Sir Josh,
Had patrons both well-heeled and posh;
    They paid him a pile,
    For they liked his Grand Style,
Which flattered them madly, by gosh.

He'd studied the Masters in Rome
For two years, and when he came home,
    Bought a splendid des. res.,
    Was the RA's first pres.,
And wrote a quite well-received tome.

Sam Johnson, the sage, was his pal,
Burke too, Boswell, Garrick, et al;
    Now he lies in St Paul's,
    And his works grace the walls
Of the Tate and the National Gall.

RON RUBIN

Said Shakespeare: "I fear you're mistaken,
If you think that my plays are by Bacon;
    I'm writing a book
    Proving Bacon a crook,
And his style an obscure and opaque 'un."

Mark Twain was a mop-headed male
Whose narratives sparkled like ale;
    And this Prince of the Grin
    Who once fathered Huck Finn,
Can still hold the world by the tale!

A vain old Professor of Greek
Would boast: "I am surely unique;
The rude hoi-polloi
All cause me no joy."
So he formed himself into a clique.

RON RUBIN

Van Gogh, feeling devil-may-care,
Labelled one of his efforts "The Chair".
No-one knows if the bloke
Perpetrated a joke,
Or the furniture needed repair.

Far beyond all the girls of Pirelli
Are the females of S Botticelli,
Each with porcelain skin
And a pert little chin,
And erogenous botti and belli.

There once was an artist called Pat
Who carried her paints in her hat;
Friends said: "It appears
From the state of your ears,
That your ultramarine is squashed flat!"

MARGARET GALBREATH

Said the Duchess of Alba to Goya:
"Paint some pictures to hang in my foyer!"
   So he painted her twice:
   In her clothes, to look nice,
And then in the nude to annoy her!

Prince Hamlet thought Uncle a traitor
For having it off with his mater;
   Revenge Dad, or not?
   That's the gist of the plot,
And he did – nine soliloquies later..

S.J. SHARPLESS

For his Campbell's Soup screen-prints, society's
Wild about Warhol. In quiet he's
   Wishing that Heinz
   Had inspired his designs –
He'd have 57 varieties,

BILL GREENWELL

"Monsieur Gauguin? E's gone to Tahiti,
Where ze girls are so friendly and preety;
   'E paints them *tout* bare,
   Wiz zair lovely black 'air,
And bodies so – 'ow you say? meaty!'"

S. J. SHARPLESS

I know of a writer of prose
Who slept with a peg on his nose;
The object, he said,
Was to keep in his head
Any thoughts that he thought in repose.

There existed a writer in clay
Whose tablets have meaning today;
His words to his peers
That survived all these years?
"No milk for this week – we're away".

A poetic rodent named Rouse
Who resides in a small country house,
Is wary of fame,
So, instead of his name,
He signs himself anonymouse.

REG LYNES

Van Gogh groaned: "This will wreck my career!
My best subject is no longer here.
The sunflowers, my pride,
Have all gone and died!"
And, despairing, he cut off his ear.

Michaelangelo moaned: "My head's reeling,
And my back and my arms have lost feeling.
I knew I would rue it,
Why on earth did I do it –
Paint the whole of that damn chapel ceiling?!"

A painter whose work you must know,
Though it's never been seen in a show,
Spends much of his time
Painting neat yellow lines
On the roads around Bromley-by-Bow.

There was an old writer called Reuel,
Whom everyone thought was a fool;
Till he wrote some huge novels
About hobbits in hovels,
And now he's a literary jewel.

The model, preparing to pose,
On seeing the artist, just froze;
Senor Pablo Picasso
Said to the young lass: "Oh,
May I have a word in your nose?"

There was an old man from Montrose
Who had a vast wart on his nose;
The wart was the sort
That inspired great thought,
And was fêted in poems and prose.
CHARLOTTE MCBEE

Said an artist: "I'll throw a big party!
You may come if you're anything arty."
Being what he liked most,
He served baked beans on toast,
Now the guests have become arty farty!

Some mates once invited Shakespeare:
"Join us for a tankard of beer!"
  Will answered: "Why, sure,
  Just a few minutes more,
While I finish the end of King Lear."

Such a shame for Apollo, I thought,
When the workmen who shifted him caught
  And broke off his penis,
  From malice or meaness,
And shipped him to England with naught.

To Chaucer the Primate said: "Shame!
To think that those Tales brought you fame;
  The issue is vital:
  Please, find a new title –
You're giving the town a bad name!"
FRANK RICHARDS

There's a wonderful family called Stein:
Why, there's Gert and there's Ep and there's Ein;
    Gert's poems are bunk,
    Ep's statues are junk,
And, well – nobody understands Ein!

There's an ignorant chap in Cape Race
Whose mind is an utter disgrace;
    He thinks Marie Corelli
    Lived long before Shelley,
And that Wells is the name of a *place!*

We was took by our teacher, Miss Beecham,
To see statues in't British Museum;
    Us girls was in fits
    Cos the int'resting bits
Of the boys was broke off – you should see 'em!

R. Crusoe said to D. Defoe:
"There is something I'd like you to know –
    Though Man Friday is sweet,
    He's not quite up my street;
Let me give that Moll Flanders a go!"

When requested to pose in the nude,
And not wishing to sound like a prude,
   I gave a small cough
   As I took my clothes off –
This story to be continued…

A miserable poet called Wally
Badly wanted to write something jolly;
   He tried and he tried,
   But he cried and he cried –
He was naturally just melancholy.

CHARLOTTE MCBEE

The Impressionist artist Cézanne
Vowed: "I'll not paint according to plan;
   My marvellous creations?
   Instant inspirations –
I just slap on the paint when I can!"

In Pinter's new play that's now running,
Our Harold's lost none of his cunning;
   Throughout the three acts,
   We hear just four facts,
But the pauses between are quite stunning!

Victoria said: "We've no quarrel
With Shakespeare, but this is immoral!
His *Measure for Measure*
Incurs our displeasure –
We don't do such things at Balmoral!"

They said: "It's high time you began
To stop playing and act like a man;
You have to grow up,
You silly young pup."
"Quite impossible!" said Peter Pan.

FRANK RICHARDS

The famous Dutch painter Vermeer
Was always so full of good cheer;
His son said: "Oh, Pappy,
You always look happy!"
It must be the Heineken beer!

As Shakespeare grew older and mellow,
He became a forgetful old fellow;
He was never quite clear
If he'd written MacLear,
Or The Two Wives of Henry Othello!

The Canterbury Tales, for sure sir,
Were written by one Geoffrey Chaucer;
His spelling was lousy,
Like "doghter" and "hous', he
Wrote some stories clean, others coarser.

A Professor of English, called Shorter,
When interviewed by a reporter;
Was asked why he chose
The study of prose,
And replied: "Sorta thought I oughta!"

A revered old writer called Maugham
Was seldom, if ever, off-faugham;
His work was incisive,
And often derisive,
But deep down his heart was quite waugham.

A curator, on quite a good salary,
Who's employed at the National Gallery,
Is so positive that
Reubens' ladies are fat
Because no one was counting the calories.

Hans Andersen went on a spree,
And came home at a quarter past three;
His wife, all irate,
Screamed: "Why are you late?
And fairy tales won't do for me!"

FRANK RICHARDS

There was a young poet called Sean
Who published an "Ode to the Dawn";
The poem was brief,
But the footnotes – good grief!
Went on for twelve pages (yawn, yawn).

ANNA KARENINA
In the works of a woman called Anna,
A handsome young blade throws a spanner;
Though she goes off the rails
When the enterprise fails,
She ends up in the opposite manner.

Mrs Malaprop nurtured an animus
Towards drunkards she thought pusillanimous;
When they drank too much port,
She suggested they ought
To join Alcoholics Unanimous!

In the country, the graceful Miss Muffet
Perched her delicate self on a tuffet;
Though the birds and bees charmed her,
A spider alarmed her –
"If that's Nature," she said. "You can stuff it!"

Having rid Hamelin Town of its vermin,
And been tricked by a noddy in ermine,
He lured girls and boys
With his pipe's pleasant noise –
Where they went, not a soul can determine.

TED THOMPSON

When Shakespeare was writing Macbeth,
His wife never stopped to draw breath;
She screamed: "There should be
Not two witches, but three!"
If there weren't, he'd have been nagged to death.
FRANK RICHARDS

An exciting young poet named Keats
Was renowned for his dare-devil feats;
He'd dance and he'd sing,
Then belch "God Save The King" –
He was very well paid for repeats.

There's an author who lives in Belsize
Who believes he is clever and wise;
Well, what do you think?
He saves gallons of ink
By simply not dotting his 'i's!

"To be," or perhaps, "not to be."
That's young Hamlet's great soliloquy;
Though he tries to suggest
He'll do what he thinks best,
It sounds like indecision to me!

Showbiz Limericks

"I shall star," vowed a girl from Biloxi,
"At Twentieth-Century Foxi!"
And her movie career
Really took off last year –
She's in charge of the mops at the Roxy.

A famous theatrical actress
Was her best in the role of malefactress;
Yet her home life was pure,
Except, to be sure,
The occasional scandal, for practice.

A convincing young actress once said,
As she gobbled down slices of bread:
"If I eat one more crust,
I am sure I shall bust,"
And, at this point, her audience fled!

A variety agent named Lou
Said: "What's this ugly old dog of yours do?"
"He juggles and sings,
And, amongst other things,
Does a perfect impression of you!"
REG LYNES

James Bond is an agent, I've heard,

Who boasts he can pull any bird;
But his date for tonight
Is a cute transvestite –
I'm sure he'll be shaken, not stirred!

There was a young lady called Mary
Who worked through the day in a dairy;
When she'd finished the milk,
She dressed up in fine silk,
And performed as a pantomime fairy.

JOE SPALDING

I knew a provincial old actor
Whose hobby was driving a tractor;
Whilst spreading the muck,
He remarked: "Luv-a-duck!
This is just like that stuff from Max Factor."

A violin player from Delhi
Believed he was Stephane Grappelli;
   When he fractured his bow,
   And gave dancing a go,
He fancied himself as Gene Kelly.

Some amateur players, most brave,
A performance of *Hamlet* once gave;
Said a wag: "Now, let's see
If it's Bacon or he –
I mean Shakespeare – who's turned in his grave."

When Randy appeared on "Big Brother"
(His manly main feature uncovered),
   He thought: "Good for me –
   On my TV CV!"
But it quite shocked his elderly mother!

Screamed the crowd to an actor named Rouse:
"Hoi! Speak up! You're as quiet as a mouse."
So he roared out with feeling,
And shattered the ceiling –
The first time he'd brought down the house!

FRANK RICHARDS

There was a magician from Stoke
Whose tricks entertained many folk;
    But, to their dismay,
    He vanished one day,
Leaving only his top hat and cloak.

A troupe of brave actors from Bray
Staged an outdoor performance one day;
    But their plans were upset
    When the weather turned wet,
And they had to declare: "Rain stopped Play"!

At a dreadful B movie sat Stan
Right behind a huge eighteen-stone man;
    He said; "Sorry, old bean,
    But I can't see the screen."
"You're lucky!" a voice said, "I can!"

A young paparazzo named May
Took a shot of a film star one day;
    When he tetchily said:
    "You have cut off my head!"
She replied: "You look better that way."

One night a magician named Matt
(Who kept his small change in his hat),
Tried to buy chocolate mousse,
But could only produce
Several rabbits, some doves and a cat!

The actress said: "Bishop, my dear,
You are standing too close to my rear."
The Bishop said: "Miss,
The view's absolute bliss –
My, the mountains are ever so clear!"

I'm appearing in Panto this year,
Though the part I'll be given's not clear;
I am game for the Dame,
Or the Prince (whatsisname?),
Or the pantomime horse (front *or* rear)!
CHARLOTTE MCBEE

Said an artiste from Barrow-in-Furness:
"The stage lights are that bright they may burn us –
You'll see, in my Sand Dance,
And my wife's Eastern Fan-Dance,
How brown they're beginning to turn us!"

Musical Limericks

A hard-drinking mezzo soprano
Got stoned at La Scala, Milano;
As they dragged her outside,
"To hell with," she cried,
"Mens sana in corpore sano!"

RON RUBIN

Says world-famous Ludwig van B:
"I've written in every damn key;
But now that I'm deaf –
E minor or F?
It's much of a muchness to me!"

RON RUBIN

Said an avant-garde jazzman called Jess,
When asked to explain his success:
"I suppose it's my sound."
(Ed: Like cats being drowned)
"And technique." (Ed: Another fine mess...)

RON RUBIN

There was an old Sikh of New Delhi
Who modelled himself on George Melly;
He'd the voice and the smile,
And sartorial style,
But he couldn't quite manage the belly.

RON RUBIN

A little-known fact about Liszt,
That listeners may well have missed:
He played ludo and lotto,
While partially blotto,
But he had to be pissed to play whist.

There was a young GI called Sherman
(Who'd once played the flugel with Herman);
"You gotta play bugle!"
Said the bandmaster, "Flugel
Is out of the question – it's German!"
RON RUBIN

A game young musician named Cager
Has, as the result of a wager,
Consented to fart
The entire oboe part
Of Mozart's Quartet in F major.

A baritone star of Havana
Slipped awkwardly on a banana;
He was sick for a year,
Then resumed his career
As a promising lyric soprana!

There's a diva in Long Island City
Whose contours are impressively pretty;
She is often addressed
By the title "Beau Chest"
Which is thought to be terribly witty.

A drunken old drummer from Devon
Expired and ascended to Heaven;
But he cried: "This is Hades!
There are no naughty ladies,
And the pubs are all shut by eleven!"
RON RUBIN

"I once played the bass," said Veronica,
With the world-famous Wigan Symphonica,
But the spike was so sharp it
Made holes in my carpet –
So I sold it and bought a harmonica."
RON RUBIN

The stinkiest animal ever
Is the pig and, despite my endeavour
To find something smellier,
The nearest I tell yer
Is a punk-band lead-singer named Trevor!
NOEL FORD

In a panic, the great prima donna
Cried: "My beautiful voice is a goner!"
But a cat in the wings
Thought: "I know how she sings."
And completed the solo with honour.

A tone-deaf old duffer from Tring,
When somebody requested he sing,
Decreed: "It is odd,
But I cannot tell 'God
Save The Weasel' from 'Pop Goes The King'!"

A lady who lived near Loch Ness
Was asked in a quiz: "Can you guess
The Queen's favourite tune?"
She ventured: "Blue Moon"
But the answer was "Corgi & Bess"!

RON RUBIN

There was a young girl with a voice
So terrible friends had no choice:
They recorded her squawking,
She heard herself talking,
And now she is silent – rejoice!

My grandpa plays bass and euphonium.
My grandma plays horn and harmonium.
My father plays flute.
My mother plays lute:
Imagine – complete pandemonium!

RON RUBIN

Some charming selections from Strauss
A pianist played at our house;
    Though we shouted "Encore!"
    And clamoured for more,
The neighbours did nothing but grouse.

Ricardo, a globe-trotting Roman,
Is quite an incredible showman;
    He'll sing "Carolina
    In the Morning" in China,
And then he'll play "Rome in the gloaming."
RON RUBIN

A person of taste in Aruba
Played a highly unusual tuba;
    When they asked: "From Peru?"
    She said: "No, Timbuktu!"
It's a regular timbuktutuba.

One night at a wild Irish Ceilidh,
A visiting Yank, called Bill Beilidh,
    Cried "Gee! What a band –
    It's so goddam bland,
I'm glad I grew up with Bill Heilidh!"
RON RUBIN

As Mozart composed a sonata,
The maid bent to fasten her garter;
   Without any delay,
   He started to play
Un poco piu appassionata.

          A charming contralto named Hannah
          Was caught in a flood in Montana;
             As she floated away,
             Her beau, so they say,
          Accompanied her on the piannah.

      There once was a tenor vibrato
      Who sang an extensive rubato;
        The start was staccato,
        The middle, legato,
      The finish – a rotten tomato!

Tchaikovsky composed his "Swan Lake",
With his grand reputation at stake;
   So he wasn't too fond
   Of its nickname "Duck Pond" –
He considered that name a mistake.

There was a trombonist called Herb
Whose playing, though loud, was superb;
When neighbours complained,
Young Herbert explained:
"But great art is *meant* to disturb!"
RON RUBIN

There was a young singer called Tess
Who sang with more force than finesse;
When she reached for top C,
It sounded to me
Like the cry of a bird in distress.
RON RUBIN

A hopeless street busker in Bute
Played some tunes on a rusty old flute;
I really can't say
If he got a bouquet –
But the listeners threw plenty of fruit!
FRANK RICHARDS

There is a musician named Long
Who's composed a new popular song;
I'm convinced it's the croon
Of a lovesick baboon,
With occasional thumps on a gong.

A lady guitarist of Bude
Was asked: "Can you play 'In The Mood'?"
She replied: "Why not? Sure!"
But her hearing was poor,
And she stripped off and strummed – in the nude!

RON RUBIN

Italians love Paganini,
Puccini and Signor Rossini,
    But lately I've found
    They're more thrilled by the sound
Of an expertly-tuned Lamborghini.
RON RUBIN

There was a composer named Liszt
    Whose music was hard to resist;
When he swept the keyboard,
    Not a listener was bored,
And now that he's gone, he is mizst.

There was an old crooner called Christie,
Who once got so terribly pissed he
    Performed the same song
    The whole damn night long
(Which may or may not have been "Misty").
RON RUBIN

There's a tone-deaf young lady, Louise,
    Who can yodel in four different keys;
Says her mother, despairing:
    "It's quite beyond bearing –
She sounds like a pack of banshees!"

A pygmy once purchased a drumkit,
Then found that he just couldn't hump it;
His arms were too short
For the trombone he bought,
So he finally settled for trumpet.

RON RUBIN

On Verdi, Giuseppe, I'm keen:
His name, if you know what I mean,
Quite rolls off the tongue
(It can almost be sung) –
A pity it just means Joe Green.

RON RUBIN

Said Handel: "Please, don't call me Herr,
I'm really quite British – so there –
And please, ven I croak,
I vould like, for a joke,
A coffin marked 'Handel', with care".

RON RUBIN

There was a young man from Dunoon
Whose bagpipes were so out of tune,
When he played a lament,
Every eardrum was rent,
And only the deaf were immune.

A musician who lived in Caracas,
Virtuoso at playing maracas,
   Said: "Although my vibrato
   Is somewhat staccato,
My maracas are absolute crackers!"

There once was a great prima donna
Whose co-star leaped madly upon her;
   "Let's do it!" he cried,
   "Sure thing," she replied,
"But right here, on stage, I don't wanna!"
RON RUBIN

There was an old drummer called Briggs
Who kept a baboon in his digs;
   He taught it "Take Five",
   And how to talk jive,
And it carried his drumkit to gigs.
RON RUBIN

A large orchestra caused quite a fuss
When it labelled its maestro a wuss;
   Though it's easy to see
   From the poor chap's CV,
He's more used to conducting a bus!

As the Spice Girls gyrated on stage,
Poor Posh moaned: "I'm feeling my age;
  I ain't no Madonna,
   Me voice is a gonner."
"Old Spice!" cried the crowd, in a rage.

"My girlfriend would like me to ski,"
Said the flabby young cellist, "But, gee!
  With Stravinsky, Stokowski,
  Mussorgsky, Tchaikovsky –
That's quite enough skiing for me!"

A boozy young student called Twist
Used to dream he could play like Franz Liszt;
  He'd got the technique,
  But his will-power was weak,
And you can't play like Liszt when you're drunk.

RON RUBIN

A musical lady named Glenda
Accompanied herself on suspender;
  The twanging elastic
  Is really fantastic,
The songs so romantic and tender.

An opera star named Maria
Always tried to sing higher and higher,
Till she hit a high note
Which got stuck in her throat –
And she entered the Heavenly Choir.

An androgynous chappie called Peake
Had a range which was surely unique:
He sang bass and contralto,
Soprano and alto,
But his treble was more like a shriek!
RON RUBIN

A tenor who hailed from Lepanto
Was known for his splendid *bel canto*;
But as for his *lieder*,
His German, dear reader,
Was rather like bad Esperanto!

RON RUBIN

A small hairy dog from Pirbright
Would sit at the organ all night;
And in this shrewd way,
He kept burglars at bay,
For his Bach was much worse than his bite!

A tone-deaf old crooner of Bray
Sang for twenty-four hours a day;
His grotty Pavarotti
Drove everyone potty –
No wonder they've locked him away!
FRANK RICHARDS

A talented dancer from Langho
Is an expert performing the tango;
To say that his waltz
Is as good would be faltz –
But he does a half-decent fandango!

A musical chap, named McDoon,
Plays the bagpipes, but never in tune;
Cats always join in
With this terrible din,
And the neighbours are moving out soon!

There was an old jazzman called Wood
Whose playing was not very good;
He idolized Louis,
But his "Cornet Chop Suey"
Was much more like "Trumpet Rice Pud"!
RON RUBIN

An unusual chap said to me:
"I am hungry for music, you see!"
He devoured a drum,
And a euphonium,
Then consumed a piano-for-tea!

The conductor, Sir Peregrine Patton,
Bruised his bald head whilst wielding his baton;
It caused him such pain,
He said: "Never again!"
And performs ever since with his hat on.

Said the leader to the vocalist Pat:
"We're way into overtime – drat!
How fast d'you suppose
You can sing 'Vie En Rose'?"
Well she did it one minute – flat.

RON RUBIN

A duff old bassoonist called Holt
Made even strong maestros revolt;
he drove Barbirolli
Clean off his trolley,
And once made Sir Adrian bolt.

RON RUBIN

Medical Limericks

A student at college named Breeze,
Weighed down by BAs and Litt Ds,
Collapsed from the strain
For, alas it was plain
She was killing herself, by degrees.

An unpopular youth of Cologne
With a pain in his stomach did moan,
He heaved a great sigh,
And said: "I would die,
But the loss would be only my own."

A two-toothed old gent from Arbroath
Gave vent to a blood-curdling oath;
When a tooth chanced to ache,
By an awful mistake
The dentist extracted them both!

There once was a man from Algiers
Who tried growing corn in his ears;
When the temperature rose,
He leapt to his toes –
Now popping is all that he hears.

There was an eccentric old boffin
Who observed, in a fierce fit of coughing:
"It isn't the cough
That carries you off –
It's the coffin they carry you off in!"

There was a young lady of Twickenham
Whose boots were too tight to walk quickenham;
    She wore them in style,
    But, after a while,
She tore them both off and was sickenham!

                An optimist, living at Datchet,
                Attempted to shave with a hatchet;
                    When his nose he did sever
                    He chortled: "I'll never
                Have nasal catarrh – I can't catch it!"

A layabout living in Rhyl
Had tried ever so hard to be ill;
    But he couldn't get rabies,
    Or buboes, or scabies –
The best he could manage? A chill!

       Each morning my wife likes to hector me
        To have an expensive vasectomy;
          But the Doc says: "Look, Fred – it
            Just ain't done on credit:
       You'll first have to write out a cheque to me!"

               RON RUBIN

A psychiatrist fellow from Rye,
Went to visit another close by,
　　Who said, with a grin,
　　As he welcomed him in:
"Hullo, Smith! You're all right. How am I?"
STEPHEN CASS

A mosquito was heard to complain
That a chemist had poisoned his brain;
　　The cause of his sorrow
　　　Was Para-dichloro
　　　　Diphenyltrichlorothane.

There was an old cynic who said:
"Though I don't despise colds in the head,
　　I get no real thrill
　　Till I'm dangerously ill,
With my friends eating grapes round the bed."
ALLEN M LAING

There was an old drunk called Heironymus
Who joined Alcoholics Anonymous;
　　But with liver disease,
　　The shakes and DTs,
The prognostication is ominous.
RON RUBIN

Hypochondriacs, father and son,
Are Mister and Master McDunne;
Every day for their ills
They take dozens of pills,
And they rattle whenever they run.

The eminent General Mago
Was a martyr to chronic lumbago,
   But gained some relief
   From undercooked beef,
Washed down with hot water and sago.

A greedy young woman from Stoke
Gobbled Big Macs and started to choke;
   The Heimlich manoeuvre
   Did much to improve her,
Along with a free can of coke.

An impotent chap from Niagara
Completed a course of Viagra;
   Instead of erectile,
   He found his projectile
Had shrunk, due to chronic pellagra!

I know a purveyor of pills
Who insists, when he uses his skills,
   His tablets and potions
   And linctus and lotions
Will cure every one of our ills.

An adventurous maiden, Antonia,
Whilst on holiday in Cephalonia,
    Sunbathed in the nude,
    Which was not only rude,
But resulted in chronic pneumonia!

Good health is more precious than riches,
But a nagging thought bothers me, which is:
    If the best treatment's laughter,
    Then, when we're looked after,
Will some doctors keep us in stitches?

My absence from bed was recorded;
Misdemeanour that promptly afforded
    Reprimand from my nurse
    And, alas, even worse,
As a punishment I was re-warded!

There was an old fellow of Spain,
Whose leg was cut off by a train;
    When his friends said: "How sad!"
    He replied: "But I'm glad –
No more trouble with varicose veins!"

An unfortunate fellow called Iestyn
Has fifty-five feet of intestine;
Though a signal success
In the medical press,
It isn't much good for digesting.

There was a young farmer from Slough,
Who said: "I've a terrible cough;
Do you think I should get
Both the doctor and vet?
Or would one be sufficient for nough?"

Whenever he got in a fury, a
Schizophrenic from Upper Manchuria
Had Pseudocyesis,
Disdiadochokinesis
And Haemotoporphyrimuria

An eccentric old lady of Honiton
(Whose behaviour I once wrote a sonnet on),
Has now been in bed
With a chill, it is said,
For a week, with her boots and her bonnet on.

There's a sensitive type in Tom's River
Whom Beethoven causes to quiver;
    The aesthetic vibration
    Brings soulful elation,
And is also quite good for the liver.

I went to the doctor's last night,
Rather hoping she'd help with my plight;
I said, whilst bent double:
"It's wind that's the trouble."
And what did she give me? A kite!
REG LYNES

Said a mournful old man of South Hill:
"Every morning I take a green pill;
    It gives me bronchitis,
    The gout and gastritis,
But, without it, I'm sure I'd feel ill!"
FRANK RICHARDS

An unfortunate lady of Lydney's
Quite well-known for her oversized kidneys;
    Should you mention their size,
    She'd exclaim.with surprise:
"They're like peanuts compared to our Sidney's!"

There's an arthritic lady in Fakenham
Whose joints have a worsening ache in 'em;
Her pain level's rising,
Which isn't surprising –
She's got pills, but hasn't been taking 'em.

An excitable fellow named Pelling;
Screamed: "On my face there's a terrible swelling!"
His doctor said; "Rot!
You silly young clot –
It's only your nose, stop your yelling!"

FRANK RICHARDS

A cannibal friend, I regret,
Has gone down with a stomach upset;
The doctor said; "Bill,
I can guess why you're ill –
It must have been someone you ate!"

RON RUBIN

A competitive surgeon from Boulder
Removed his own arm (at the shoulder),
Then repeated the feat
With one hand on both feet –
The record stands, though not the holder!

There was a young lady from Looe
With a terrible dose of the flu;
She wheezed and she coughed
Till her poor head fell off –
Watch yourself! It might happen to you.

An old gourmet who'd grown rather stout,
Felt a twinge and considered the gout:
" I shall imbibe," He thought,
"Several bottles of port –
That is certain to settle all doubt!"

A frail fellow, sickly at best,
Was subject to colds on his chest;
For years he'd endured it,
But finally cured it
With a twelve-volt electrical vest!

A sneezing chap left his abode,
And avoided his friends in the road;
When they questioned him: "Why?"
His considered reply
Was: "I dode wad you cadgin by code!"

He was ogling a pretty girl when
A huge steamroller hit Uncle Ben;
In the hospital they
Wrote a label: "Long Stay" –
He's in wards number 8, 9 and 10!

The optician spoke to young May:
"I shall give you an eye-test today;
Your eyes, I suspect,
Have at some time been checked?"
Said May: "No, they 'ave always been grey!"
RON RUBIN

There was an old man in a hearse
Who thought: "I have never felt worse!
This box is quite roomy,
Though dark and so gloomy –
Is it too late to send for the nurse?"
REG LYNES

Job's comforters now are emphatic
That his illnesses – whether rheumatic,
Sclerotic, arthritic,
Myopic, paralytic –
Were, quite simply, psychosomatic.

An athletic young rambler from Clewer
Once incited a bull to pursue her;
But she vaulted the gate
Just a fraction too late –
Now when she sits down, she says: "Oo-er!"

There was aince an auld body o'Sydney
Wha suffered frae pains in the kidney;
He prayed tae the Lord
That he might be restored,
And He promised He would – but He didnae!

Historical Limericks

Tutankhamen, best known as old Tankh,
Was a Pharoah of infinite rank;
But his sarcophagus
Wouldn't cause all this fuss
If his name had been Freddie or Frank.

ELSIE RIDGEWELL

Archimedes, the early truth-seeker,
Leaping out of his bath, cried: "Eureka!"
And ran half a mile,
Wearing only a smile,
Thus becoming the very first streaker.

S.J. SHARPLESS

George Stephenson said: "These repairs
Are costing a fortune in spares;
I'll be out of pocket
When I've finished this Rocket,
Unless British Rail raise their fares."

FRANK RICHARDS

Wee Jamie, a canny young Scot,
Observed, when the kettle was hot,
That the steam raised the lid,
And it's thanks to this kid
That you and I both know Watt's watt.

JOYCE JOHNSON

Two earnest young fellows named Wright
Discovered the secret of flight;
   Now the eager young crew
   Of a B52
Can wipe out the world overnight!
BASIL RANSOME-DAVIES

"Come now," said Bell, "this is choice:
The first telephone! Let's rejoice!"
Now listen folks, all,
To the very first call:
"Sorry, number engaged." said a voice.
FRANK RICHARDS

Marconi, whose ardour was tireless,
Sat down and invented the wireless;
Which makes it less tough
For the musical buff
Who lives in a town that is choir-less.

S. J. SHARPLESS

A crusader's wife slipped from the garrison,
And had an affair with a Saracen;
   She was not over-sexed,
   Or jealous, or vexed –
She just wanted to make a comparison.
OGDEN NASH

Said Wilbur Wright: "Oh, this is grand,
But Orville, you must understand,
We've discovered all right
The secret of flight –
The question is, how do we land?"
FRANK RICHARDS

It is clear that Napoleon's Queen
Was referring to army routine,
When she said, in a flummox:
"*Marchons-nous sur nos* stomachs?"
And was told: "Not tonight, Josephine!"
MOSS RICH

The trouble with General Sherman,
He acted too much like a German –
Attacking Savannah
In much the same manner
As Adolf or Heinrich or Herman.
BASIL RANSOME-DAVIES

What led to the crassness of Custer
With hardly a unit to muster?
At the Little Big Horn,
Sitting Bull gave a yawn,
And said: "You're a sitting duck, buster!"

Said Wellington: "What's the location
Of this battle I've won for the nation?
They replied: "Waterloo."
He said; "That'll do.
What a glorious name for a station!"

FRANK RICHARDS

George Washington said to his dad:
"You know that big fruit-tree you had?
I've just chopped it down.
Now, father, don't frown –
I cannot tell a lie. Aren't you glad?"
FRANK RICHARDS

Isaac Singer (you probably know)
Had ambition his business should grow;
But inventors before him
A few grudges bore him,
And thought him a right sew-and-sew.

A clumsy young schoolgirl called Bessy
Had to write on the Battle of Cressy;
As she sat down to think,
She knocked over the ink,
Bessy's essay on Cressy was messy.
FRANK RICHARDS

The Wright Brothers, dreaming of levity,
Made a flight of nonsensical brevity;
The engine's bad shudder
Was caused by the rudder,
And threatened the couple's longevity.

"It's gravity" I. Newton said,
When an apple fell down on his head;
But, oh, what dismay
On that memorable day
If Gran Smith had dropped on him instead.

Said Guy Fawkes: "I am willing to bet
I could blow up this Parliament yet;
The powder's all right,
But I can't strike a light,
Because all of my matches are wet!"
FRANK RICHARDS

James Watt one fine morning in Spring,
Watched the kettle boil over and sing;
He said, with regret:
"I'd invent a train yet,
If I could only put wheels on the thing!"
FRANK RICHARDS

To the castle the raging hordes thundered
(Local scribes say about seven hundred),
But Attila the Hun
Was just having some fun,
And only the Gift Shop was plundered.

There once was a Hun, named Attila,
Whose life was a genuine thrilla;
   From village to village,
  He'd rant, rape and pillage,
Seldom spending two nights on one pilla!

     King Canute sat alone on the beach
     And observed as each wave followed each;
     When they lapped at his boots,
     He thought: "That's it, old fruit!
     They have won, now get out of their reach!"

The immaculate Sir Walter Raleigh
Had a terrible row with his valet,
   Who, on seeing his cloak,
   Cried: "You lousy old soak,
You've been rolling about in some alley!"
FRANK RICHARDS

Newton, experimenting in Pisa,
Dropped fruit (soft) from aloft on a geezer;
   The man cried: "Depravity!"
   Said Newton: "No, gravity –
But don't worry, the apple is free, sir!"

When Cromwell went out on parade
He inspected each troop and brigade;
And, whenever he found
That a head was not round,
He smoothed out the bumps with a spade.

The Romans had, so it appears,
IV limbs and I nose and II ears;
The toes of these men
All numbered X,
And they lived LX months in V years.

Godiva, the lass with long hair,
Had to ride on a horse whilst quite bare;
So she let her hair down
As a substitute gown,
And gave the horse blinkers to wear.

There once was an old Roman ogre
Who took up the practise of yoga;
He twisted and bent,
But could not prevent
Getting tied up in knots in his toga.

Growled William: "Just watch while I fix
These Saxons (up to their old tricks):
    They'll remember the year
    That I arrived here!"
And they have – it was 1066.

"This is gravity," Newton had said,
When an apple dropped down on his head;
But judge the dismay
On that memorable day
If a brick had dropped on him instead!
FRANK RICHARDS

The caves in the Stone Age were dusty,
And chilly, and draughty, and musty;
But surely much worse
Was the terrible curse
Of the Iron Age, with everything rusty!

Said birthday boy Midshipman Mick,
On the *Marie Celeste*'s final trip:
"I was hoping I'd get
A Conjuring Set –
Let me show you this vanishing trick!"
REG LYNES

A couple of fellows named Wright
Messed about in the shed, day and night;
The hammering sound
Made the rumours abound,
Until they emerged and took flight.

Great Kings of Peru were the Incas,
Who were known far and wide as great drincas;
They worshipped the Sun,
And had lots of fun,
Though their enemies thought they were stincas!

Checking up every hour on the hour,
Said Noah: "Where's my reckoning power?
According to me,
We are on the Black Sea,
But we've just passed the Post Office Tower!"

Miscellaneous Limericks

A thrifty young fellow of Shoreham
Made brown paper trousers and woreham;
He looked nice and neat
Till he bent in the street
To pick up a coin, then he toreham.

There once was a knight called Sir Bert
Who said: "Oh. this armour does hurt!
I can stand it no more;
Nip down to the store
And fetch me a non-iron shirt."

GERARD BENSON

A vain polar bear known as Lilly,
Liked clothes that were flimsy and frilly;
    She swapped her thick fleece
    For a lacy two-piece,
So she's chic but exceedingly chilly.
JULIA RAWLINSON

There was a young lady named Rose
Who had a huge wart on her nose;
    When she had it removed,
    Her appearance improved,
But her glasses slipped down to her toes.

A painter who lived in West Ditting
Interrupted two girls with their knitting;
    He said, with a sigh,
    "That park bench – er, well, I
Have just painted it, right where you're sitting!"

When she bought some pyjamas in Cheltenham,
A lady was asked how she felt in 'em;
    She said: "Winter's all right,
    But on a hot night
I'm afraid that I might even melt in 'em."

A mariner rounded Cape Hope
Whilst daydreaming of soap-on-a-rope:
  "Six months on this tub,
  I could do with a scrub!"
But the chance of a decent wash? Nope!

A cry-baby-bunting from Italy
Was booing and hooing quite bitterly;
His mamma said: "Pooh!
Wass a-matter a-you?"
He replied: "Some a-dog a-just bit a-me!"

There was a young fellow named Tom
Who invented a large home-made bomb;
  If you need dynamite,
  Consult his website:
Blowupandtakecover.com.
PAM GIDNEY

The ankle's chief end is exposiery
Of the latest designs in silk hosiery;
Also, I suspect,
It's a means to connect
The part called the calf with the toesiery.
ANTHONY EUWER

Cried Frankenstein's Monster: "By heck!
I feel like a physical wreck!
   My face has more stitches
   Than two pairs of britches,
And these bolts are a pain in the neck!"

WILLIS HALL

There was a young man of Montrose,
Who had pockets in none of his clothes;
   When asked by his lass
   Where he carried his brass,
He said: "Darling, I pay through the nose."

ARNOLD BENNETT

There once was a diarist named Pepys
Who wrote about London in heaps;
   When the Fire had died down,
   Pepys went about town,
And culled tales that give one the creeps.
HUGH POWELL

As a beauty I am not a star:
There are others more handsome, by far;
   But my face – I don't mind it,
   For I am behind it –
It's the people in front get the jar!
H. WOODROW WILSON

There was a young fellow of Ceuta
Who rode into church on his scooter;
   He knocked down the Dean,
   And said: "Sorry, old bean!
I ought to have sounded my hooter!"

A candid professor confesses
That the secret of half his success is
Not his science, as such,
Not its marvels so much
As his bright and intuitive guesses.

THOMAS THORNELEY

There was an old person of Florida
Whose conduct could not have been horrider;
At his hotel, the waiters
He pelted with taters,
And the chambermaids kissed in the corridor,

LANGFORD REED

A bricklayer's oppo named Porter
Got steadily shorter and shorter;
The reason, he said,
Was the hod on his head,
Which was filled with the heaviest mortar.

Though your dreams may seem normal and right,
They bring horrible things to the light;
    You can only be sure
    That you're perfectly pure
If you dream about nothing all night.
J. C. B. DATE

The mate of a fast-sinking freighter
Knelt down and besought his Creator:
    "O, Lord, stem the tide!"
    To which God replied:
"I can't chum – I'm just a spectator!"
RON RUBIN

There was a young Japanese Geisha
Who suffered from mild alopecia;
She met a young Briton,
Identically smitten,
And they now run a barber's in Esher.
RON RUBIN

There was a young lady named Hannah
Who slipped on a peel of banana;
    More stars she espied,
    As she lay on her side,
Than there are in the Star Spangled banner.

A baffled young housewife from Kent
Said: "I'm brassic, I haven't a cent.
   I've made just two stops
   In a couple of shops,
But I'm blowed if I know where it went!"

A radical curate from Brent,
Who gave up entirely for Lent,
   Just lay in the aisle
   With a faraway smile,
And dreamt of The Duchess of Kent.

There was an old rich man of Notts,
Did he have enough money? Yes, lots!
   He'd his own private train,
   Plus a large aeroplane,
And several magnificent yachts.

There was a young lady named Josie
   Whose uncle's proboscis was rosy;
When she questioned him: "Uncle,
     Is that a carbuncle?"
He replied, with a sniff: "Don't be nosey!"

In Paris some visitors go
To see what no person should know;
    And then there are tourists,
    The purist of purists,
Who say it is quite *comme il faut*.

An inexact lad, Alexander,
Once called an old lady a gander;
    Said she: "You mean goose –
    I'll not stand such abuse!"
And she took out a summons for slander.

Julie, a friend of a friend,
Cleaned lavatories at the weekend;
    Whenever she rushed,
    She'd get awfully flushed,
And was thought to be clean round the bend.

There was an Archdeacon who said:
"May I take off my gaiters in bed?"
    But the Bishop said: "No,
    Wherever you go,
You must wear them until you are dead!"

At Gray's Inn, a student of law
Has declared legal jargon a bore;
Is there anything dafter
Than to say "hereinafter".
And "whereas" and "heretobefore"?

There was a great Marxist called Lenin
Who did two or three million men in;
That's a lot to have done in,
But where he did one in,
That grand Marxist Stalin did ten in.
ROBERT CONQUEST

I saw in this morning's *Express*
Prince Charles in a transparent dress;
Oh – is that the Royal Show?
The Queen shouted: "No!"
But the man from Del Monte said: "Yes!"

There was a young lady named Alice
Who peed in a Catholic chalice;
The padre decreed
Twas done out of need,
And not out of Protestant malice.

"I must leave here," said Lady de Vere,
"For these damp airs don't suit me, I fear."
Said a friend: "Goodness me!
If they do not agree
With your system, don't *eat* pears, my dear!"

A newspaper writer named Bing
Could make copy of most anything;
    But the copy he wrote
    Of a ten-dollar note
Was so good he is now in Sing-Sing.

There was a young lady of Bandon
Whose feet were too narrow to stand on;
    So she stood on her head,
    "For my motto," she said,
"Has always been *nil desperandum*."

A young Irish servant in Drogheda
Had a mistress who often annogheda;
    Till she finally swore
    In a language so raw,
That thereafter nobody emplogheda.

There was an obstreperous minx
Who, when asked what she thought of the Sphinx,
Replied, with a smile,
"That old fraud by the Nile?
Well, personally, I think she stinx!"

A renegade priest from Liberia
Whose morals were clearly inferior,
　Once did to a nun
　What he shouldn't have done,
And now she's a Mother Superior.

An insistent Archbishop named Ddodd
Had manners determinedly odd;
He said: "If you please,
Spell my name with four "d's!"
Although one was sufficient for God.

A keen social climber from Crewe
Enquired: "What on earth shall I do?
　I, of course, know what's what,
　But I fear I have not
Got the faintest idea of who's who!"

Said the venerable Dean of St Paul's:
"Now, regarding these cracks in the walls –
Do you think it would do
If we filled them with glue?"
But the Bishop of Lincoln said: "Balls!"

An adventurous damsel from Brighton,
Whom nothing could possibly frighten,
    Plunged into the sea
    And, with infinite glee,
Was seduced by a playful old Triton.

There was a young lady called Harris
That nothing would ever embarrass;
    Till the bath-salts one day
    In a tub where she lay
Turned out to be plaster-of-Paris!

OGDEN NASH

A plumber from Lowater Creek
Was called in by a dame with a leak;
    She looked so becoming,
    He fixed all her plumbing,
And he didn't emerge for a week!

A hirsute young chap from St Paul's,
Who reads *Harper's Bazaar* and *McCall's*
    Has developed such passion
    For feminine fashion,
That he's crocheted a snood for his balls!

A suspicious cashier in Calais
Kept accounts which, reviewed, did not talais;
Soon his boss smelled a rat,
For he'd furnished a flat,
And was seen, every night, at the balais!

It's strange how the newpapers honour
The creature that's called Prima Donna;
They say not a thing
About how she can sing,
But write reams of the clothes she has on her.

Two eager and dashing young beaux
Apprehended and robbed of their clothes,
Will not mind a lot
While the weather is hot,
But what will they do if it snows?

Said the Mate, of a sailboat that creaked,
To the Captain: "What port shall we seek?"
Said the Captain: "We'll dock her
In Davy Jones' Locker –
This ancient old tub's sprung a leak!"

There was a young lady from Trent
Whose TV antenna got bent;
The neighbours went crazy:
Their screens became hazy,
For, instead of receiving, she sent!

He received, from some thoughtful relations,
A spittoon with superb decorations;
When asked was he pleased,
He grimaced and wheezed:
"It's beyond all my expectorations."

When she took that proud walk down the aisle,
She was dressed in the latest of style;
But a friend later said
With a shake of her head,
That her petticoat hung down a mile.

Our heroine fled to Bermuda,
Where her lover, young Gerhard, pursued her;
When he begged her: "Be mine!"
And she answered him: "Nein."
Every man in the audience booed her.

There once was a student named Bessor
Whose knowledge grew lesser and lesser;
It at last grew so small,
He knew nothing at all –
And today he's a college professor!

The fabulous Wizard of Oz
Retired from magic becoz
What with up-to-date science,
To most of his clients
He wasn't the wizard he woz.

There was an old farmer from Reece
Who used to throw things at the geese;
   One day, just for fun,
   He threw cakes and a bun,
Four erasers, a dog and his niece!

There was a young monarch called Ed,
Who took Mrs Simpson to bed;
   As they bounced up and down,
   He said; "Bugger the crown!
We shall give it to Albert instead!"

The man that they dubbed JFK
Was shot by Lee Oswald, they say…
   An open and-shut-case?
   Or some other nutcase –
Well, what were *you* doing that day?
RON RUBIN

A poetess, luscious and slim,
Indulged an unusual whim:
When composing a sonnet,
She affected a bonnet,
But stripped herself bare for a hymn.

There was an old man of Khartoum
Who kept two ugly sheep in his room;
"They remind me," he said,
"Of two friends who are dead."
But he never identified whom.

There was a young chap so benighted,
He didn't know when he was slighted;
    He went to a party,
    And ate just as hearty
As if he'd been really invited.
FRANCES PARKINSON KEYES

"Princess," said the Frog, "Do not wince!
I'll convince you I'm really a Prince."
    So he changed into tights,
    And demanded his rights,
And nobody's heard of him since.
GINA BERKELEY

A glib little beer-buff from Troon
Says slim girls will cause him to swoon;
    A girl with no waist
    Is of course to his taste,
With his gut like a busted balloon.
BILL GREENWELL

A cute secretary, none cuter,
Was replaced by a clicking computer;
    'Twas the wife of the boss
    Put this deal across,
You see, the computer was neuter.
OGDEN NASH

I once knew a spinster of Staines,
And a spinster that lady remains;
    She's no figure, no looks,
    Neither dances, nor cooks –
And, most ghastly of all, she has brains.
PLAIWON

Said a tripper: "Oh, joy, to have found
Such a glory of sight and of sound!
   How our heart-strings are stirred
   By the song of a bird,
As we scatter our litter around!"
THOMAS THORNELEY

Jack, who had no airs and graces,
Would leap upon folk from high places;
   But his end came about
   When he jumped with a shout,
And was caught on a branch by his braces!

Life is sad and so slow and so cold
As the leaves that were green turn to gold;
   As the lonely lake fills,
   And there's ice in the hills
And the long loathly Winter takes hold...
GAVIN EWART

There was an Old Man with a Beard
Who said: "I demand to be feared;
   Address me as God
   And love me, you sod!"
And Man did just that, which is weird.
ROGER WODDIS

The Chief Stewardess on a Boeing
When asked where the aircraft was going,
    Said: "Our navigator
    Is joining us later,
And, till then, we have no way of knowing.
PAUL ALEXANDER

A lady on climbing Mount Shasta
Complained when the mountain grew vaster;
    It wasn't the climb,
    Or the dirt, or the grime,
But the ice on her ass that harassed her.

The reason we're asked to endure
A gutter press, smutty, impure,
    Is that old river Fleet,
    Whose name's on the street,
Is an ordurous, underground sewer.
BILL GREENWELL

Said an eminent, erudite ermine:
"There is one thing I cannot determine –
    When a dame wears a coat,
    She's a person of note –
When I wear it, I'm deemed only vermin."

A millionaire, filled with elation,
At his newspaper's wide circulation,
    Said: "With murder, divorces,
    And hints about horses,
I am moulding the mind of the nation."
THOMAS THORNELEY

I'm getting deep lines on my forehead;
My face is becoming quite florid.
    I measure with dread
    My middle-aged spread –
I think growing old is quite horrid.
RON RUBIN

Rupert Murdoch, with glee, shouted: "What
A lot of newspapers I've got!
    I've just got to get
    The *Beekeeper's Gazette*,
And *The War Cry*, and I've got the lot!"
FRANK RICHARDS

At a Fête a small fellow named Spence,
Through misfortune and gross negligence,
    Got mixed up with the jumble,
    But what made him feel humble –
He was sold for just twenty-five pence!

On her birthday a girl from Dumbarton
Received in the post a large carton;
   It contained a big cake
   From which burst a rich sheik –
The very thing she'd set her heart on.

A girl called Miss Fortune sighed: "Oh,
My name's a misfortune, I know;
   Miss Take's just as bad,
   Miss Fitt is quite mad,
And that Miss B Haviour must go!"

Do you know that policeman's address?
No, I don't but I'll have a good guess:
   With pride I've espied
   Where most coppers reside –
999 Letsbe Avenue. Yes?

There was a young woman of Notts
Who, when learning Morse Code, cried out: "What's
   The matter with me?
   Dashes fill me with glee –
But I can't get along with the dots."

There was a young lady of Oakham
Who would steal your cigars and then soak 'em
In treacle and rum,
With a coating of gum,
So it wasn't so easy to smoke 'em!

Said a gentle old chap: " I suppose
I ought not to wear my best clothes,
    But, what can I do?
    I have only two –
And these are no better than those!"

There once was a Sultan named Fairham
Who liked to play tricks on his harem;
    He captured a mouse
    He set free in the house,
And called the result Harem-Scarem!

An unfortunate girl in Havana
Slipped on a discarded banana;
    Away went her feet
    As she took a seat
In a very unladylike manner!

The rock group got up on the stage
(Just beginning to show their old age);
    They played through the night,
    One guy said: "We're shite!
But we have to pretend we're the rage!"
MARGARET BRACE

There was a young lady named Stella,
Fell in love with a bow-legged fella;
    The venturesome chap
    Let her sit on his lap,
And she fell down clean through to the cella.

There was an old lady named May
Who played with her false teeth all day;
    When they fell on her plate,
    She cried out: "I hate
Mithaps of thith kind, may I thay!"

A dizzy old duffer named Topping
Fell down fifty-five flights without stopping;
    The janitor swore
    As old Top hit the floor:
"This will take me the whole darn day mopping!"

"Ah, Goldilocks!" said father Bear,
"I've been looking for you everywhere;
    I want ten pence, my pet,
    For that porridge you ate,
And I've got a small bill for a chair..."

An heiress from Abergavenny
Had offers of marriage (so many),
    She surveyed all the men
    Very gravely, and then
Said: "Well, no thanks, I'm not having any!"

There was an old man of Darjeeling
Who travelled from Tottenham to Ealing;
    It said on the door:
    "Please don't spit on the floor."
So he carefully spat on the ceiling.

There was an old spinster from Wheeling
Endowed with such delicate feeling,
   She thought any chair
   Shouldn't have its legs bare,
So she kept her eyes fixed on the ceiling.

There was a young lady of Kent
Who always said just what she meant;
   People said: "She's a dear,
   So unique and sincere!"
But they shunned her by common consent.

There was a young lady named Snood
Who was such an insufferable prude,
   That she'd pull down the blind
   When changing her mind –
Lest a curious eye should intrude!

A teacher from Leamington Spa,
Announced to her ma and her pa:
   "A boy whom I taught,
   Is a brave astronaut –
I always knew he would go far!"

There was a young bather called Mark
Who spotted the fin of a shark;
   He said: "The deep sea
   Is no place for me!"
And retired to the pond in the park.

There was a young lady of Denbigh
Who wrote to her confidante: "NB:
   I don't mean to try
   To be married, not *I* –
But where can the eyes of the men be?"

A mischievous maiden from Shoreham
Stole some clothes of her brother's and wore 'em;
   But her family said,
   As they put her to bed,
That it showed a great want of decorum!

O God, forasmuch as without Thee
We are not enabled to doubt Thee,
   Help us all by Thy Grace
   To convince the whole race
It knows nothing whatever about Thee.
RONALD KNOX

There was an old man from Dumfries
Who was stung on the nose by some bees;
   He uttered loud cries
   As it swelled to the size
And the colour of ripe Edam cheese!

A minister sat on some holly,
Put there by a choirboy (what folly);
He leapt from the pulpit
In search of the culprit,
And soon made him rue it, by golly!

An old men's-outfitter named Bert
Had a tip he believed was a cert;
   But the horse came in last,
   And poor Bert was aghast:
"Oh, gor blimey, there goes my last shirt!"

There was a gravedigger from Barnes
Whose clothes were all covered in darns;
   He'd dug fewer holes
   In his life, for poor souls,
Than his sweater had under the arms.
MICHAEL PALIN

There was an old Welshman called Morgan
Who had a magnificent organ;
Said his wife: "You are blessed
With the absolute best
Hammond Organ in all of Glamorgan!"

RON RUBIN

The drinks left for him by each bed,
Had gone straight to old Santa's head;
   He was found off the road,
   With an upside-down load,
And himself slumped, dead drunk, in his sled!

An old lady who lived at Lake Wales
And consumed only oysters and snails;
   Upon growing a shell,
   Remarked: "It's just as well –
Now I've no need of bonnets or veils."

Two beauties who dwelt by the Bosphorus
Had eyes that were brighter than phosphorous;
   The Sultan cried: "Troth!
   I shall marry you both!!"
But they laughed: "We're afraid you must toss for us!"

No matter how grouchy you're feeling,
You'll find a smile more or less healing;
   It grows in a wreath
   All around the front teeth,
Thus preventing the face from congealing.

There was a young lass from Dundee
Whose knowledge of French was "Oui, oui";
   When they asked: "Parlez vous?"
   She replied: "Same to you!"
A superb bit of fast repartee.

Said a chap to his wife in East Sydenham:
"My trousers! Pray, where have you hiddenam?
   It is perfectly true
   They are hardly that new –
But I've foolishly left thirty-quidenham!"

There was a young lady from Lancashire
Who once went to work as a bank cashier;
   But she scarcely knew
   One and one equals two,
So they advertised for a young man cashier.

A classical scholar from Flint
Has developed a curious squint:
   With one of her eyes
   She'll be scanning the skies,
Whilst the other's perusing small print.

There was a young fellow called Priestly,
Whose behaviour to women was beastly;
   He'd promise them wine,
   And a jolly good time –
Them give them a weekend in Eastleigh.
MICHAEL PALIN

A churchman, austere and refined,
Said: "This age most permissive I find;
   Nakedness on TV
   Does not bother me –
It's the staying up late that I mind."

The Irish are great talkers,
Persuasive and disarming;
   You can say lots and lots
   Against the Scots -
But at least they're never charming!
GAVIN EWART

I took a short holiday flight
That landed in Spain late at night;
But my cases I found
Were all Far Eastern bound,
And my language was far from polite!

I met a young man from Korea
Who had a prosthetic new ear;
   He could swivel it round
   To capture all sound

From the front or the sides or the rear.
In Loch Ness a monster once stayed,
Thus boosting the Scots tourist trade;
   When it disappeared
   (For ever it's feared),
The locals were left quite dismayed.

"Dear Mother," wrote wee Diggie Broon,
"I've dug a hole thirty foot doon;
   I'll dig and I'll toil,
   Until I've struck oil."
She sent him a card: "Get Well Soon!"

A reluctant Italian grocer
When invited to climb Monte Rosa,
    Remarked to his wife:
    "No thanks, not on your life!
I've got anoraksia nervosa!"

I put all my eggs in one basket,
Saved a password (lest someone should ask it),
    But my banker went bust,
    And now I have just
Enough money to purchase a casket.

A health-concious Rector named Jessop,
To exercise chooses the press-up,
    Or walking the dog,
    Which is more of a slog,
And also involves clearing mess up!

My computer has gone on the blink.
If I knew why, I'd fix it (I think);
    A dialogue box
    Looks at me and mocks –
Technology stinks! Bring back ink!

A Wizard and Witch were surprised
When they turned themselves into mince pies;
Someone else in the coven
Popped them into the oven,
Which led to their early demise.

Britain hopes to be able quite soon
To dispatch its first man to the moon;
But will said astronaut
Become truly distraught
When his suitcase arrives in Rangoon?

A chap who ascended to Heaven
Arrived twenty-five past eleven;
When he rattled the gate,
Peter said: "You must wait –
We are closed till tomorrow, at seven!"

The neighbours from Hell live next door.
The noise starts at something to four:
The barking of dogs,
Or the screaming of sprogs,
Or the drill – I can't *stand* anymore!
CHARLOTTE MCBEE

There was an old man of Hong Kong
Who never did anything wrong;
   He became an MP
   And behaved honourably –
But I don't think he held the job long.
FRANK RICHARDS

An inquisitive student from Dorking
Worships at the feet of S. Hawking;
   She knows the brief history
   Of each cosmic mystery,
But has an odd manner of talking.

An incompetent plumber from Goole,
Fixed new pipes in the town swimming pool;
Now the shallow end's hot,
But the deep end is not,
And the bit in between's always cool.

There was a young lady from Chester
Who worked as a steamroller tester;
   But she made up her mind
   It was time she resigned –
Having found that the job so depressed her!

There's a ghost on the Isle of Wight
That haunts an old mansion at night;
   Should you meet on the stairs,
   You will find that the hairs
On the back of your neck stand upright!
CHARLOTTE MCBEE

There was an old fellow from Shoreham
Who would buttonhole people and bore 'em;
   If he chose to attend,
   Any meeting would end
With the sudden collapse of the quorum.

We are left in a state of near trauma.
They insist that we're all getting warmer;
   But whenever I'm told,
   I'm invariably cold,
And would settle right now for the former.

"I shall melt in your warm arms," he told her,
Still he couldn't resist just to hold her;
   He succumbed to the heat
   And collapsed at her feet –
He was only a chocolate soldier.

It may be of interest to know:
If your income is average or low,
That early-rise bakers
(Our staff-of-life makers),
All appear to make plenty of dough.

There was an old person of Wilts
Who would stride about town upon stilts,
    Looking smart in all sorts
    Of long trousers, or shorts,
But was careful to never wear kilts.
FRANK RICHARDS

A useless mechanic named Sutch
Did a hopeless repair on a clutch;
    In first gear up to top
    The car coughs to a stop,
And in neutral it moves, but not much.
REG LYNES

As a practising sit-on-the-fencer,
I am neither a for-or-againster;
    But I make firm decisions
    (With essential provisions),
From a viewpoint that's left/right of centre.

I know an old man of Durazzo -
I've never known anyone chat so!
From the time he's begun
Till the moment he's done,
I can only say: "Really! Is that so?"

The poker game got very heated
When the players thought someone had cheated;
   They cursed and they swore
   Until they were sure,
Then they called him… Expletive Deleted!

     In developing submarine doors,
    Engineers have invented a pause –
      Rushing water might freeze
      As it swirls round the knees,
So there's time to don waterproof drawers.

Said a very plump girl from Devizes,
When summoned before the Assizes,
   For stealing, to wear,
   A marquee from the Fair:
"But no-one sells large enough sizes!"

A fatso called Derek from Wales,
The same size as several small whales,
   Hung around like a slob,
   Till he landed the job
As a windbreak on beaches in gales.

There's a grouchy old farmer near Neath
With an ill-fitting set of false teeth;
   When there's ramblers about,
   He's quite likely to shout:
"Bugger off! Or I'm fetching the Pleeth!"

A small Bed and Breakfast in Crete
Offers several nice rooms (all en suite);
   If you don't mind the food,
   Or the landlord, who's rude,
You can stay till the end of the week.

An electrical shop in Two Bridges
Has an offer on: purchase two fridges,
   Get a chest freezer free,
   A machine that makes tea,
And a gadget that's lethal to midges!
REG LYNES

A grumpy old gardener called Quorn
Is feeling quite sad and forlorn;
A pack of foxhounds
Burst into his grounds,
And destroyed his immaculate lawn!

A chap on a diet of fruit
Has grown far too thin for his suit;
   Although Granny Smith may
   Keep the doctor away,
The Grim Reaper's in hot pursuit!

A Tory bod out in his motor,
Ran over a Labourite voter;
   "Thank goodness!" he cried,
   "He was on the wrong side –
So I don't blame myself one iota!"

There was a young chap at the War Office
Whose brain was no good as a store office;
   Every warning severe
   Simply went in one ear,
And out of the opposite orifice.

There was an old fellow of Tyre
Who constantly sat on the fire;
   When asked: "Aren't you hot?"
   He said: "Certainly not!
I am Charles Winterbottom, Esquire!"

Oh, the Lib-Dems are searching the land for
The breakthrough they've long hoped and planned for;
　What gets in their way
　Is that not even they
Have the slightest idea what they stand for!

There's an old Irish word meaning "thief" –
Four letters, quite pithy and brief:
　I tell you no lie,
　It is T-O-R-Y,
Now doesn't that beggar belief!

The spy who came in from the cold,
Muttered: "Now that I'm getting so old,
　I would like to enlarge
　On this espionage,
But I can't write my memoirs, I'm told."

I think our Quiz Team may be cursed.
Out of all local pubs we're the worst;
　Those questions last night –
　We got every one right,
Still out of twenty, we came twenty-first!

A clever young farmer called Max
Is avoiding the gasoline tax;
It's so simple, you see,
For his Chevvy burns pee
From his grandfather's herd of tame yaks.

A lady who'd been to the Lizard,
And thought that the Lizard was wizard,
   Had heard that the view
   Was remarkable too –
But she couldn't see much for the blizzard!

My weird older sister, Anita,
Is a regular well-known man-eater;
   She enjoys them the most
   Served with honey on toast –
It makes them taste such a lot sweeter.

A young scout named Benjamin Potts
Saw a snake attack two tiny tots;
   In a nonchalant way,
   Benny snatched it away,
And then used it to practise his knots.
NOEL FORD

Eighty-seven-years-old Mrs Brown
Wears false teeth when she's shopping in town;
   She asked in one shop
   For; " ˙doɥɔ ʞɹod ʎʇɐǝɯ ∀ "
She was wearing her teeth upside down!

A cross English teacher, stern-faced,
Said: "This class is an utter disgrace;
  Your diction is poor:
  Just look at the floor –
Dropped aitches all over the place!"

I've heard of a servant, though civil,
Who talks nothing but absolute drivel;
  He advises the men
  In Downing Street (Ten) –
If all changes, he's ready to swivel.

An adventurous lady named Hall
Wore a newspaper dress to a Ball;
  The dress caught on fire,
  And burned the entire
Front page, sporting section, and all!

A model called Susie Du Bar
Has committed a dreadful *faux pas;*
  She loosened a stay
  In her décolleté,
Thus exposing her *je ne sais quoi* !

There was an old crusty mechanic
Whose manners were fierce and tyrannic;
    Dull headlights would glare
    At his furious stare,
And dead engines turn over in panic!
N. M. BODECKER

An old school bus-driver from Deering
Disconcertingly kept disappearing;
    He would head for Cape May,
    But end up in Bombay,
Because something was wrong with the steering.
N. M. BODECKER

Some travellers lugging valises
Said: "Sir, could you tell us where Greece is?"
    When he said: "But I'm Swiss."
    They said: "Then tell us this –
How do you make holes in your cheeses?"
N. M. BODECKER

A tiresome person in Corning
Just would not get up in the morning;
    When they said: "Tell us why."
    She made some reply,
Though they couldn't hear what for her yawning.

This middle-aged person from Keene
Is neither too fat nor too lean,
    Not too good, not too bad,
    Neither happy nor sad,
But content to be somewhere between.

This far-roaming lass from Milwaukee
Walked all the way to and from Gorki;
    They admired her walk,
    But said: "Boy, does she talk –
That unstoppable Milwaukee-talkie!

There was a young fellow of Acre
Who took off his cap to a Quaker;
    When the worthy man said:
    "You are very well-bred."
He replied: "But of course – I'm a baker!"

There was a young fellow called Taft
Who sailed out to sea on a raft;
    Some thought him daring,
    Their praise was unsparing –
While others considered him daft!

There was an old man of Lucerne
Who didn't like waiting his turn;
"All this standing in line –
You may think it is fine,
But you won't find a bus queue in Berne!"

There is an old lady called Lottie
Whose face is inclined to be spotty;
That isn't so bad,
But what's really sad
Is her mind is decidedly dotty!

A scrap-metal merchant called Clanger
Kept an ancient old car in a hangar:
"My very first choice
Would be a Rolls Royce,
But I'm settling for an old banger!"

There was a man in Atchison
Whose trousers had rough patchison;
He'd often state
He found them great
To scratch his parlour matchison!

There once was a fellow called God
Whom everyone thought rather odd;
Apart from a lady
Called Eileen O'Grady
Who worshipped the ground that he trod.

MICHAEL PALIN

An ambassador based in the East
Who'd invited a sheikh to a feast;
 Had the shock of his life,
 For he'd said: "Bring your wife."
And the sheikh brought two dozen – at least!
FRANK RICHARDS

Sherlock Holmes, a remarkable man,
Took one glance at a rusty old can,
   And said: "It's quite clear
   This was opened last year,
By a bald-headed dwarf, from Japan!"
FRANK RICHARDS

One Saturday morning young Mike
Took his rod and went fishing for pike;
   But he came home distraught,
   For all that he'd caught
Were six boots and a rusty old bike!

A boy with an extra-large bite
Sadly swallowed his favourite kite;
   Too many beans (tinned)
   Always give him such wind,
After supper, he's bound to take flight!

An overweight lady from Chertsey
Met the Queen and attempted to curtsey:
   "I do hope this will do –
   I am nineteen-stone-two,
And to bend any lower just hurts me!"

A quick-witted sailor from Skye
Admits with a wink in his eye:
   "Whenever I get
   My bell-bottoms wet,
I ring 'em until they are dry!"

When the teeth of a lady called Wodgem
Came loose as she rode on a dodgem,
   And fell into her jumper,
   Though other cars bumped her,
They totally failed to dislodge 'em!

A little old person of Nigg
Displayed a most far-reaching wig;
   When they said: "You're too small."
   He replied: "Not at all –
It's the wig, I suspect, that's too big!"
N. M. BODECKER

A splendiferous person of Haxey
Whose mustaches were pointy and waxy,
   Tied flags, left and right,
   (And small lanterns at night)
To the points when he travelled by taxi.
N. M. BODECKER

A star-gazer, full of much bonhomie,
Was extremely well-versed in astronomy;
   But his study of Mars
   Made him think of snack bars –
Now his new expertise is gastronomy!

There is an old biddy called Whitehouse
Who lives by herself in a lighthouse;
   Storms rage every night,
   And the light is so bright,
She's not certain she's chosen the right house.

A learned professor from Jackson.
Once honked at a cop with his klaxon;
   When sternly admonished,
   The professor astonished
The cop with some choice Anglo-Saxon!

There was an old Aussie called Short
Who shot kangaroos, just for sport;
   When caught and arrested
   And tried, he protested:
"This is nought but a kangaroo court!"

There was an old cowhand called Jess
Who played a real mean game of chess;
   When his partner called: "Checkmate!"
   He growled; "Check? The heck, mate!"
And shot him (such lack of finesse).

There was an old Sultan of Saudi
Who rose up one morning and vowed he
   Would take a new wife,
   To embellish his life –
"For the others," he said, "Are so dowdy!"

There was a stout lady of Dorset
Who couldn't unfasten her corset;
   So she called the police, who
   Said: "We can't release you –
Perhaps a good locksmith could force it?"

A cheerful old cowboy called Rudy
Is never bad-tempered or moody;
   He'll greet you with: "Hey,
   Pardner – whaddaya say?"
Or sometimes just "How d'you doody!"
RON RUBIN

There was an old lodger called Gissing,
Whose landlady came at him, hissing:
   "Have you taken a bath?"
   Stepping out of his path,
He replied: "God forbid! Is one missing?"
RON RUBIN

There was a young girl from Connecticut
Who wasn't too well-versed in ecticut;
   When asked out to dine,
   She upset her wine,
And mopped it all up with her pecticut!

RON RUBIN

When had up for pilfering, Percival
Entreated the judge: "Please, be merciful!"
   But the judge thundered: "Percy,
   I'll show you no mercy –
My sentence is quite irreversible!"

A considerate Abbot of Nice
Was so fond of his old Renault Six,
   When it gave up the ghost,
   He said: "Friends, let us toast
This noble machine – rust in peace!"

A wily old burglar called Dubbs
Picked all kinds of locks, even Chubbs;
   But Dubbs came a cropper
   When he burgled a copper –
Now he's doing time in the Scrubs.
RON RUBIN

A skinny young girl of Vancouver
Was swallowed one day by a Hoover;
   She was rather dismayed,
   When the Fire Brigade
Took four or five days to remove her!

RON RUBIN

There was an old man of Cambodia
Who said to his wife: "Did you know, dear,
   Our country, I hear,
   Was once called Kampuchea?"
She replied: "Well, it just goes to show, dear!"

There was a young sailor called Mort
Who didn't know starboard from port;
   "Nor can I," he laughed,
   "Tell the fore from the aft –
And, you know, I'm entirely self-taught!"

Said a spoilt senorita of Ronda,
When her mum and dad bought her a Honda:
    "I'm fond of my Honda,
    But, oh, how much fonder
I'd be of a brand new Lagonda!"

There was an old preacher called Herman
Who found people slept through his sermon;
    It wasn't his themes –
    The problem, it seems,
Was the sermon was always in German.

There was an old person of Pinner,
As thin as a lath, if not thinner,
    Who sunbathed one day,
    When a hungry young jay
Said: "Here's a nice worm!" and had dinner.
FRANK RICHARDS

A lazy housewife from Spokane,
Said: "This housework is really a pain –
I dust, sweep and wash,
Then in six months, by gosh,
The whole place needs doing again!"

A little boy, all on his tod,
Composed a short poem to God:
   He said: "Dear Jehovah,
   My dog is called Rover."
God answered: "Mine too. That *is* odd!"

A poor, homeless lady in Shrivenham,
Who'd a new pair of shoes with no give in 'em,
   Thought: "I'll stretch them a touch."
   But she stretched them too much –
And now they're so big, she can live in 'em!

Quoth a wise man from Afghanistan:
"If I ran and I ran and I ran,
   As the world's but a ball,
   Well, in no time at all,
I'd be right back here where I began!"

A sleepy old chap from Penrose,
Whose loud snores interrupted each doze,
   Now sleeps undisturbed,
   For his snoring is curbed
By a clothes-peg he's clipped to his nose.

A young country lass in Kentucky
Led a lifestyle a little bit mucky:
 She squatted in pens,
 Pulling feathers off hens –
Still you'd have to admit, she was plucky!

When Lady Penelope Thrupp
Invited a dustman to sup,
 Her butler observed
 Not: "Dinner is served."
But, in manner disdainful: "Grub's up!"

A Queen with a crown of dull pewter,
Grew steadily glummer, and muter;
 "Why can't she have gold?"
 Asked a courtier, bold,
"Because," said the King, "It don't suit 'er!"

A disgruntled, plump shopper in Kent
Made this rather inventive lament:
 "Not one dress could I find
 That would fit my behind,
So I'll have to convert this – a tent!"

I admit that it may look like greed,
But it's not fish and chips that I need;
   Yes, I buy them each day,
   But I throw them away,
And just keep the paper to read!

A chap we met in Singapore
Was the most irritating old bore;
   He had us all yawning
   Till four in the morning
With stories we'd all heard before.

A sage said: "To walk is pedestrian,
And riding a horse is equestrian;
   But stay in one spot,
   And squat in a pot,
And you may call yourself aspidistrian!"

An incurable gambler named Fetter
Was quite shocked when accused as a debtor;
   At the bookmaker's shop,
   He insisted he'd stop
"Ten to one I'll reform, and get better!"

A charming young lady named Nelly
Once danced herself almost to jelly;
The doctors declared
That her life might be spared
If she stayed for a week in Pwllheli.

A pious old monk named Carruthers
Had a beard so much longer than others;
So this generous monk
Kindly cut off a chunk,
And has knitted hair shirts for the Brothers.

A well-endowed lady from Bude
Went bathing one day in the nude;
From the lifeguard a shout:
"Oi! Inflatables out!"
There was no need to be quite so rude.

A water-diviner, or dowser
Went out with his terrier Towser,
    And tripped arse over tit;
    Said the dog: "Such a twit -
You've got both of your legs in one trouser!"

When Henry the Eighth was a lad,
He announced with conviction: "Egad!
    To have only one wife
    For the rest of your life,
Would be mad. I'll have six!" And he had.

An astronaut, one afternoon,
Signalled base: "I am coming down soon:
    I've had such a fright
    From a very strange sight –
A cow jumping over the moon!"

As I typed out a letter one day,
I snapped off my capital 'A';
   WHEN I USED 'E' INSTEED,
   IT WES TOO HERD TO REED,
SO NOW I USE 'O' – HIP HOOROY!

A postman who'd never liked red,
Crept out every night from his bed;
   Soft-footed in socks,
   He'd find each pillar box,
And paint it bright yellow instead!

A dutiful train-driver, Mike,
Whose union had come out on strike,
   Went on a go-slow
   When the signal said "Go",
And was passed by a greengrocer's bike!

A skyscraper dweller named Lee
Left each morning at 8.23;
   But invariably found
   When he got to the ground,
It was time to go home for his tea!

A romantic guy from Buena Vista,
Fell in love with a flea-trainer's sister;
   Cupid's bow loosed its dart
   In a line to her heart,
But she bent down to scratch, and it missed her!

A six-foot young maiden, Miss Pooter,
Couldn't choose her most suitable suitor:
   The one ardent youth
   Was tall, but uncouth,
Whilst the other was short, but much cuter.

A nervous young fellow named Mark
Stays away from the park in the dark;
   His mum says: "Poor mite!
   Do you think trees might bite?"
He says: "No, I'm afraid of their bark."

Said a practical thinker: "One should
Help to kill superstition for good;
   I, for instance, refuse
   To observe all taboos,
With immunity, so far, touch wood!
FRANK WATSON

There was an old lady of Bickleigh
Who often looked spotty and sickleigh;
   She claimed: "It's this vest,
   It tickles my chest –
I'm sure the material's too prickleigh!"

Mostly women get married, it's true –
They must feel it's the right thing to do;
   But why spend your life
   Being somebody's wife,
When you might spend it just being you?
BARNEY BLACKLEY

A dainty soul in Albuquerque
Gets depressed when the weather is murky;
   But a ridge of high-pressure
   Will quickly refresh her,
And anti-cyclones make her perky.
FRANK RICHARDS

There was a young chap from the Hague
Whose beliefs were annoyingly vague:
   He considered zucchini
   A work by Puccini,
And Scarlatti as some sort of plague.
FRANK RICHARDS

There once was a paragon, Pearl.
My word! What an exquisite girl!
   Her acquaintances said:
   "When she grows up, she'll wed
A prosperous Duke, or an Earl!"

Though physicists get in a stew
About which assumption is true:
   That Space is expanding,
   Or steadily standing –
I don't give a bugger, do you?
RON RUBIN

Said a homeless rough-sleeper named Jones:
"I must sleep every night on cold stones;
    Pavement slabs are for treading,
    Not intended for bedding,
And, as such, are not good for my bones."

There was a young dancer called Sally
Who dreamed of a life in the ballet;
    Her fouette was a fright,
    And her tutu too tight,
So she's settled for tap at the Palais.

From his Georgian des, res. in Devizes,
The architect blueprints high-rises;
    The folk who must live in 'em
    Have never forgiven him,
Still he wins many prestigious prizes.
RON RUBIN

An old toff who drives a large Bentley,
Accelerates ever so gently
    To the outskirts of town,
    Where he puts his foot down
And tears round the countryside mentally!
REG LYNES

A man who made hats in East Filby,
Invented a fold-away trilby;
   He sewed the last stitch,
   And declared: "I'm not rich,
But give it a week and I will be!"

A ghost by the name of McGraw,
Longs to haunt room a-hundred-and-four;
   But whenever he dares
   To ascend flights of stairs,
He slips, with a sigh, through the floor.

A sadistic Head Teacher from Wembley
Would drink till his knees went all trembly;
   One day, somewhat smashed,
   He enjoyably thrashed
The rest of the Staff at Assembly.

A strapping young woman named Shirley
(In anyone's book she is burly),
Is built like a horse,
With rough hair like gorse,
And she smells not in any way girly!

A traffic-cop based in the Bronx,
Shouted: "Hey! I ain't seen ya in yonks!"
    And stood chatting to friends
    In their Mercedes Benz,
Despite all the catcalls and honks.

A one-legged spinster from Ryde
Couldn't dance but, to be fair, had tried;
    She managed a tango,
    And *half* a fandango,
But can-can? She couldn't. And cried.

A miser was driving his Rolls
When he came to the Severn Bridge tolls –
    "How much d'you require?"
    "A grand to you, squire!"
(His riposte's not for sensitive souls).

A nervous old lady said: "Hark!
There's a bear in the bush in the park!"
    And she shot up a tree,
    But the gates closed at three –
Now she's all by herself in the dark...

Said an alien, unpacking his case,
On arrival from somewhere in Space:
   "You earthlings, inferior –
   My race so superior!"
And tripped and fell flat on his face.

A bankrupt old potter from Ottery,
Won a prize in the Ottery Lottery,
That, to his surprise,
Was sufficient in size
To refurbish his Ottery Pottery.

There's a farmer from Newcastle West
Who once courted a maiden with zest,
   And so hard did he press her
   To make her say: "Yes, sir."
That he broke the old watch in his vest.

Two tourists at fair Salthill Strand
Once tried to make love on the sand;
   The policeman on duty
   Cried: "Hang on, me proud beauties –
Them foreign contortions is banned!"

A balding old chap from Bailrigg
Was considering wearing a wig;
    He complained: "It's too small!"
    They said: "No, not at all –
Your head's several sizes too big!"

An eager young chap from Fazakerley
Stops work at four-thirty exakerley;
    He opens his wages,
    And counts them for ages:
"New banknotes is so nice and crakerley!"

An illiterate chap from Much Hoole,
Nearly drowned when he fell in a pool;
    Had he not seen the warning?
    He had, every morning,
And regretted not going to school.

The weatherman stood by his map:
"The temp'ritures goin" tae drap
    In sooth west Argyll;
    Yil sune lase yir smile –
The rain will come oan like a tap!"

There was a young lady named Bright
Who travelled much faster than light;
She started one day
In the relative way,
And returned on the previous night.

There was an old Justice called Percival
Who said: "I suppose you'll get worse if I'll
Send you to jail,
So I'll put you on bail."
Now wasn't Judge Percival merciful?

At Christmas you get given socks,
Or hankies or slippers or chocs;
It's always some gift
That leaves you quite miffed –
Why can't I just play with the box?
MARGARET BRACE

In Florida, famous for fun,
A tourist lay prone in the sun;
With her lipstick she wrote,
On her tummy, a note:
"Please, do turn me over when done."

Gardening Limericks

An indolent vicar of Bray
Allowed his prize rose to decay;
   His wife, more alert,
   Bought a powerful squirt,
And said to her spouse: "Let us spray!"

A grumpy old gardener, careworn,
Was regretting he'd ever been born,
   When some unrestrained hounds
   Chased a fox through his grounds,
And quite ruined his manicured lawn.

A sensitive chap named Hawarden
Went out to plant blooms in his garden;
   If he trod on a slug,
   Or a worm, or a bug,
He'd immediately say: "Beg your pardon!"

There was an old fellow from Fyfe
Who'd been gardening most of his life;
   He dreamt, in his slumbers,
   Of giant cucumbers,
Which greatly embarrassed his wife.

A green-fingered lass named Veronica
Grew a prize-winning, bright red Japonica;
So, how did she nourish
The plant, make it flourish?
She played to it on her harmonica.

A devious gardener from Leeds
Sold packets of counterfeit seeds;
    The scam was uncovered
    (The money recovered),
When all of them came up as weeds.

She partied dressed as an Azalea,
A decision which proved such a failure;
    For troublesome Doug
    Dressed up as a bug
And chewed her entire regalia!

I've learned so much about trees and shrubs
From a number of gardening clubs;
    And also the evils
    Of aphids and weevils,
And numerous bugs and their grubs.
CHARLOTTE MCBEE

An old lady gardener of Harrow,
Whose views were exceedingly narrow,
    Put separate bird baths
    At the end of her paths
For the different sexes of sparrow.

Our garden's quite small, there's no room
For the flowers when they're in full bloom;
   So we just have the veg
   And an old privet hedge,
But we're having a bird bath built soon.
CHARLOTTE MCBEE

"Mother Earth," chant the millions of ants
On our badly beleaguered young plants,
   Whilst eating the greenfly
   "We know what you mean by
Biological Warfare – and thanks!"

There is an old gardener from Staines
Who shelters in sheds if it rains;
The unfortunate truth's
That they never have roofs,
And he gets soaking wet for his pains.

REG LYNES

My husband keeps filling his shed
With stuff I'll throw out when he's dead;
Such as hundreds of tins,
And all manner of things
Like the springs from our old double-bed!

427

A gardener who hailed from Dundee
Thought what a good joke it would be
To cross onions with roses,
And get up the noses
Of the friends his wife asked round for tea.

My husband can't wait, aftersowing,
To watch all the little plants growing:
Lots of little green shoots
With their little green roots –
Won't be long till the lawn'll need mowing!

Never shin up a hawthorn for height
If a rotweiler gives you a fright
Your best bet? Stand your ground,
For the researchers have found
That *its* bark is much worse than *his* bite!

Have you *seen* my immaculate lawn!
One small patch looks a little careworn:
Discoloured I'd say.
Sort of greenish-grey:
Rex will wish he had never been born.

Memorial Limericks

An incautious young lady of Guam
Who'd observed: "The Pacific's so calm!"
   Paddled out for a lark,
   But bumped into a shark…
Let us now sing the Ninetieth Psalm.

"He's rung his last bell," mourners cried,
When their bus-conductor friend died;
   Then the coffin lid groaned,
   And a voice within moaned:
"There's room for two standing inside!"
WILLIS HALL

There was an old man who averred
He had learned how to fly like a bird;
   Cheered by thousands of people,
   He leapt from a steeple –
This tomb states the date it occurred.

There once was an elegant Miss
Who said: "I think skating is bliss."
   This no more will she state,
   For a wheel off her skate
Made her finish up something like this!

There was a young fellow of Spa
Who yearned to become a film star;
　　So he dived, for a stunt,
　　Clad in mail from a punt –
The funeral's tomorrow. Ha! Ha!
LANGFORD REED

A singular Yankee of Wis,
Found a sleep in a hearse not amiss;
　　It sounds most perverse,
　　But he wished to re(hearse)
His ride to the ne-crop-ol-is.

An Irish roadworker named Flynn
Heard a busker beginning to sing;
　　He shouted: "You're flat!
　　We're not having that!"
But his steamroller ran over him.

A boastful young fellow of Neath,
Once hung from the roof by his teeth;
　　A very large crowd
　　First cheered him out loud,
Then passed round the hat for a wreath.
FRANK RICHARDS

Said a boastful young student from Hayes,
As he entered the Hampton Court Maze:
    "There's nothing in it.
    I won't be a minute."
He's been missing for forty-one days.
FRANK RICHARDS

A cat in despondency sighed,
And resolved to commit suicide;
She passed under the wheels
Of eight automobiles,
And under the ninth one she died.

At a bullfight in sunny Madrid,
A tourist went clean off his lid;
    He made straight for the bull
    While the crowd yelled: "You fool!
You'll go home in a box!" And he did.

A sickly young chap down in Florida
Collapsed in a hospital corridor;
    A strange nurse from Maine
    Tried to banish his pain
With a shotgun. Now, what could be horrider!

When she saw all the birds in the sky,
My sister said: "Why can't *I* fly?"
So, with paper and things,
She made herself wings,
And jumped off a clifftop. Goodbye!

Through the town went young Timothy Hyde:
"Oh, I'm dreadfully poorly!" he cried;
    When they said: "You're OK."
    Tim answered: "No! Nay!
I'm not." And to prove it, he died.

There once was a man named McBride
Who jumped down a manhole and died;
    He's never been found
    In those pipes underground,
And his end was proclaimed "sewer-cide"!

Miss Bliss and her suitor named Bell
Sat perched on the edge of a well;
    Said he: "Oh, my dove,
    I am falling in love!"
So she pushed him and, in love, he fell.

There was a young fellow named Vivian
Who had a dear friend, a Bolivian,
    Who dropped his cigar
    In a gunpowder jar –
His spirit is now in oblivion.

A silly young man from Port Clyde
In a funeral procession was spied;
Asked: "Who, pray, is dead?"
He giggled, and said:
"I don't know, I just came for the ride."

A visitor once to Loch Ness
Met the monster who left him a mess;
They returned his entrails
By the regular mails,
And the rest of the stuff by Express.

There was an old man in a hearse
Who murmured: "This might have been worse;
Of course the expense
Is simply immense,
But it doesn't come out of *my* purse!"

Sid Longbottom climbing Ben Nevis
Fell fifty feet into a crevice;
He was wedged by *ars longa*,
Recovered, got stronger,
Then passed out RIP *vita brevis*.

A jolly young fellow from Yuma
Told an elephant joke to a puma;
Now his skeleton lies
Beneath hot western skies –
The puma had no sense of huma.

OGDEN NASH

A nurseryman was most unwise
In refusing his workers a rise;
He was given a header
Right into the shredder,
And nobody mourned his demise.

There was a young fellow from Tyne
Laid his head on the railway line;
But he died of ennui,
For the 4.43
Did not come till a quarter past nine!

A new servant maid named Maria,
Had trouble in lighting the fire
(The wood being green),
So she used gasoline…
Her position, by now, is much higher.

There was a young man of South Bay
Making fireworks one fateful day;
He dropped his cigar
In the gunpowder jar…
There was no young man of South Bay.

An impetuous fellow named Weir
Who hadn't a smidgin of fear,
    Indulged a desire
    To touch a live wire…
Almost any last line will do here!

There was a young man from Tacoma
Whose breath had a whisky aroma,
So, to alter the smell,
He swallowed Chanel,
And went off in a heavenly coma.

In skydiving he found such expression,
Thus conquering his bouts of depression;
    Then one day, as he bailed,
    His parachute failed –
But he left quite a lasting impression.

The driveway was almost complete,
When she wanted it moved several feet;
    As she fell in the mixer,
    They said: "That will fix her –
From now on she'll be more concrete!"

There was a young rambler called Hilda
Who went for a hike on St Kilda;
    They say that the climb
    Is really sublime,
But not so for Hilda – it killed her!

A decrepit old gasman named Peter,
While poking around a gas heater,
    Touched a leak with his light,
    And rose clear out of sight –
And, as everyone who knows anything about
poetry will tell you, he also ruined the meter!

An adventurous gourmet from Crediton
Took *pâté de foie gras* and spread it on
    A chocolate biscuit,
    And murmured: "I'll risk it."
His tomb bears the date that he said it on.

In the turbulent, turgid St Lawrence
Fell a luscious young damsel named Florence,
    Where the poor, famished fish
    Made this beautiful dish
Into an object of utter abhorrence.

There was a young driver named Jake
Who made the most stupid mistake:
    He drove through a brick wall
    And right into the hall,
When he mixed up the gas and the brake.

There was a young man from the city
Who met what he thought was a kitty;
    He gave it a pat,
    Murmured: "Nice little cat…"
They buried his rags, out of pity.

There was a young chap from Laconia
Whose mother-in-law had pneumonia;
    He hoped for the worst,
    And after March 1st
They buried her 'neath a begonia.

Astute Melanesians on Munda
Heard a parson discussing the wunda
Of Virginal Birth –
They debated its worth,
Then tore the poor padre asunda.

A Frenchman called Didier Brume,
Had a clear premonition of doom;
So, to hasten his death,
He just held his breath,
And lay, all alone, on a tomb.

MICHAEL PALIN

There was a young man from Kilbride
Who fell into a sewer and died;
His unfortunate brother
Fell into another,
And now they're interred, side by side.

Said a widow, whose singular vice
Was to keep her late husband on ice:
　　"It's been hard since I lost him –
　　I'll never defrost him!"
Cold comfort, but cheap at the price.

There once was a Countess of Ryde
Who swam too far out with the tide;
　　Thought a man-eating shark:
　　"How is this for a lark?
Have faith, and the Lord will provide!"

Said the vet as he looked at my pet:
"That's the skinniest bear I have met;
　　I'll soon alter that."
　　Now the bear's nice and fat –
The question is – where is the vet?
FRANK RICHARDS

In memory of someone, I fear
Who drank too many pints of strong beer,
　　And walked fifty-one feet
　　In a line, straight and neat,
Off the end of a fifty-foot pier.

An old duffer was driving his car,
When his passenger said: "Dear Papa,
    If you go at this rate,
    We are sure to be late –
Please, drive faster!" He did, and they are!

There once was a fellow called Hyde
Whose twin self he could not abide;
    But Jekyll, the devil,
    Dragged Hyde to his level:
"Inside job!" cried Hyde as he died.
E. J. JACKSON

At the railway station, old Jim
Crossed over the line on a whim;
    When he crossed back again,
    He did not miss his train,
And the train, sadly, didn't miss him!

A careless bus-driver, called Ron,
Crashed the 8.45 and passed on;
    His tomb (near the bend)
    Marks his untimely end,
And has "terminus" writ thereupon.

"I'm as strong as an ox!" was the boast
Of a cocky young chap from the coast;
    "To prove it I'll now
    Lift this Hereford cow…"
His coffin's much flatter than most.

The man on the flying trapeze
Emitted a quite frightful sneeze;
    The consequent force
    Shot him right off his course –
He was found, miles away, in some trees.

Asked the marvellous illusionist, Zorro,
"Eez a girl in ze crowd may I borrow?
    My assistant's got flu:
    I shall saw you in two?" –
She'll be buried today, and tomorrow!

A bit of a nutter from Settle
Who'd eat anything made out of metal,
    Ate hundreds of pins,
    Lots of forks and some tins,
Then choked on a rusty old kettle.

A hiker, much lighter than cork,
Went out for an afternoon walk;
    She flew like a fool,
    In her wind-filled cagoule,
And crash-landed outside Mohawk!
CHARLOTTE MCBEE

                    There was an old man of Bordeaux
        (That's in France, just in case you don't kneaux),
                    Who sank in *la mer*
                    Just off Cape Finisterre
        And his last words were: *"Eau! Eau! Eau! Eau!"*

There was a young fellow named Fonda
Who was squeezed by a great anaconda;
    Now he's only a smear,
    With part of him here,
And the rest of him somewhere out yonder.

There once was a housewife of Pisa
Who carelessly fell in the freezer;
    It's not very nice
    When your spouse turns to ice,
And disposal's a bit of a teaser!

here was an old drunk of Algiers
Who quaffed eighty-seven straight beers;
    His epitaph reads
    (You must peer through the weeds):
Succinctly and simply, just "CHEERS!"
RON RUBIN

A short-sighted housewife called Jean
Read a quick way to melt gelatine;
    She applied a fierce light
    To some raw gelignite –
Since that moment she hasn't been seen.
FRANK RICHARDS

Said a butcher's apprentice from Frome,
Who aspired to be bride (and not groom):
    "With some knives from the shop,
    I'll perform my own op."
And these words are inscribed on his tomb.

Limerick
Variations

THE DOUBLE LIMERICK

THE EXTENDED LIMERICK

THE PROSE LIMERICK

THE BEHEADED LIMERICK

THE LIMERICK POEM

THE UNRHYMED LIMERICK

THE DOUBLE LIMERICK

That rebellious rodent called Jerry,
    And his chum, the cat-astrophe, Tom,
Have perpetual hatchets to bury,
    And get like a hydrogen bomb
    Whenever the feline
    Is making a bee-line
        For succulent prey
        In his truculent way
He has several bites of the cherry
    But the mouse chews him up with aplomb.
BILL GREENWELL

A fiery young fellow called Bryant
    Was struck by a maiden called May,
And though he was almost a giant,
    And she but a tiny thing, they
    Were very soon wedded,
    For both were hot-headed,
        Her first name was Vesta,
        And once he possessed her,
She turned out agreeably pliant,
    And the match has survived to this day.
BARNEY BLACKLEY

THE EXTENDED LIMERICK

There once were two cats of Kilkenny.
Each thought there was one cat too many,
So they quarrelled and fit,
They scratched and they bit,
Till, excepting their nails
And the tips of their tails,
Instead of two cats, there weren't any!

There was a strange student from Yale
Who put himself outside the pale;
   Said the Judge: "Please refrain,
   When passing through Maine,
From exposing yourself again in the train,
   Or you'll just have to do it in jail!"

He turned up in Hamelin, hell-bent to kill
Rats. When he'd killed all he meant to kill,
   He asked for his pay,
   But they told him: "No way!"
   So, feeling quite stung,
   He vamoosed with their young –
"I wish," said the Mayor, "We'd called Rentokil!"

RON RUBIN

THE PROSE LIMERICK

THE SEMANTIC LIMERICK ACCORDING TO THE SHORTER OXFORD ENGLISH DICTIONARY (1933)

There existed an adult male person who had lived a relatively short time, belonging or pertaining to St John's*, who desired to commit sodomy with the large web-footed swimming birds of the genus *Cygnus* or subfamily *Cygninae* of the family *Anatidae*, characterized by a long and gracefully curved neck and a majestic motion when swimming.

So he moved into the presence of the person employed to carry burdens, who declared:
"Hold or possess as something at your disposal my female child! The large web-footed swimming birds of the genus Cygnus or subfamily *Cygninae* of the family *Anatidae*, characterized by a long and gracefully curved neck and a majestic motion when swimming, are set apart, specially retained for the Head, Fellows and Tutors of the College!"

THE SEMANTIC LIMERICK ACCORDING TO DR JOHNSON'S DICTIONARY (Edition 1765)

There exifted a person, not a woman or a boy, being in the firft part of life, not old, of St John's*, who wifhed to ——— the large, water-fowl, that have a long and very ftraight neck, and are very white, excepting when they are young (their legs and feet being black, as are their bills, which are like that of a goofe, but

*A College of Cambridge University

fomething rounder, and a little hooked at the lower ends, the two fides below their eyes being black and fhining like ebony).

In confequence of this he moved ftep by ftep to the one that had charge of the gate, who pronounced; 'Poffefs and enjoy my female offspring! The large water-fowl, that have a long and very ftraight neck, and are very white, excepting when they are young (their legs feet being black, as are their bils, which are like that of a goofe, but fomething rounder, and a little hooked at the lower ends, the two fides below their eyes being black and fhining like ebony), are kept in ftore, laid up for a future time, for the fake of the gentlemen with Spanish titles!'
GAVIN EWART

Since R.V. Knox's ad in *The Times* (see page 39), other clever limericks have appeared in a variety of disguises. This, a sign to be displayed at a railway station ticket office:

> The train that was due to depart at 8.10 is not likely to start. We're working to rule, you'd best get a mule or a bike or a horse and a cart.

This, a sign in a clothes shop:

> When placing an order, please note that delay will be saved if you quote the style of your preference, as well as the reference number and size of the coat.

And two others, the first from the forecourt of a garage, for customers to read, the second to be hung in the workshop of the same garage, being instructions to the mechanics:

> When cars are left here for repair, our charges are modest and

fair. And owners may rest quite content that we test all work that is done with great care.

In the shed at the end of the mews there's a bucket of old bolts and screws, and right at the back you will see a large stack of old junk that perhaps you can use.

Limericks disguised as letters can make interesting reading:

Dear Doctor,
Please look at young Millie. I hope she's not done anything silly. She's been staying out late, and she's putting on weight.
Yours faithfully,
(Mrs) O'Killey

Dear Mam,
I am lernin to spel I hoap
you an dad are boath well this skool is
kwite nice but ive run away twyss
With luv from yor dorter, yung Nell

Dear Prof,
In reply to your note, we find you are far too remote. To cut out conjectures, we're cutting your lectures.
The Class
(by unanimous vote)

THE BEHEADED LIMERICK

These are very clever examples of "beheaded" limericks, written
by a Mrs Arthur Shaw, of New Orleans, many moons ago:

A nice patch of golds that were mari
Belonged to a dan who was harri;
When cals who were ras
Filled their kets that were bas,
She put up a cade that was barri.

In Gonia once, which is Pata
A clysm occurred that was cata:
A gineer who was en
Lost his ture that was den
In a torium there that was nata.
[NB A natatorium is a North American term for a swimming pool}

THE LIMERICK POEM

THE RIME OF THE ANCIENT MARINER
(After Samuel Taylor Coleridge)

A mariner collars a guest
On his way to a wedding, hard-pressed;
Bewitched and in fear,
He has to give ear
To the whiskery wild-eyed old pest.

The seafarer tells him a tale
About a stout ship that set sail
South, over the line,
And everything fine,
Till – Curses! – a force-fifteen gale!

An albatross, bird of good luck
(Which looks like a dirty great duck),
Now shadowed the ship,
Safeguarding their trip,
Till the mariner shot it, the schmuck.

Problems: the wind disappeared;
Sun-scorched, the lads blamed Greybeard;
With many a scowl,
They hung the dead fowl
Round his neck – most symbolic and weird.

The crew were by now crazed with thirst,
And the old sailor knew they were cursed;
Then on the horizon
He clapped his mad eyes on
A ship – and his heart nearly burst!

This ship, alas, turned out to be
A phantom. On board they could see
Death and Death's Mate
Playing dice for their fate;
The upshot: all perished but he.

Remorseful, he lay on the deck,
A pitiful, gibbering wreck;
Then he started to pray,
And the curse flew away –
And the albatross fell from his neck.

Then rain came, and wind like a whip,
And the Dead rose to man the tall ship –
A skeleton crew,
But they knew what to do –
And the vessel moved off at a clip.

Well, to cut a long story quite short:
The Fates became bored with their sport;
They called it a day,
Sped the ship on its way,
And somehow it limped home to port.

The vessel was now neither spick
Nor span, and it sank double-quick;
But a pilot's boat raced
To the rescue, post haste,
And the old salt was saved in the nick.

Now a hermit, who lived in a wood,
Near the harbour, was Holy and Good;
The sailor confessed,
And the hermit, impressed,
Absolved him as best as he could.

Yet still, as a penance, he must
Drift round this planet like dust,
And make a career
Out of bending the ear
Of folk, who are often nonplussed.

He exits on uneven keel,
And the guest, though in need of a meal
And some booze, opts to ease up
And bypass the knees-up,
Which somehow has lost its appeal.

RON RUBIN

SUMMER
(Written at the age of thirteen-and-a-half, as a "prep" exercise)

Whatever will rhyme with Summer?
There only is "plumber" and "drummer":
Why! the cleverest bard
Would find it quite hard
To connect with the Summer – a plumber!

My Mind's getting glummer and glummer
Hooray! there's a word beside drummer;
Oh, I will think of some
Ere the prep's end has come
But the rhymes will get rummer and rummer.

Ah! If the bee hums, it's a hummer;
And the bee showeth signs of the Summer;
Also holiday babels
Make th'porter gum labels.
And whenever he gums, he's a gummer!

The cuckoo's a goer and comer
He goes in the hot days of Summer;
But he cucks ev'ry day
Till you plead and you pray
That his voice will get dumber and dumber!

SIR JOHN BETJEMAN

TESS OF THE D'URBERVILLES
(after Thomas Hardy)

This is the story of Tess,
Whose life was a bit of a mess;
Seduced by a lad
Called Alec, by gad –
She doesn't take long to say "Yes".

An infant is born nine months later:
It dies without meeting its pater,
Who scarpers, the jerk,
And Tess goes to work
On a farm, where a new chap will date her.

This clergyman's son, Angel Clare,
Says: "Tessie – our lives we must share!"
But the night of the wedding,
Bang there in the bedding
She tells him about her affair.

So Angel takes flight, crying: "Shame!
You women are all the damn same!"
And Tess, in adversity
(Or female perversity),
Goes back to Al, her old flame.

Alec has meanwhile found God,
But still likes his fun, crafty sod;
And Tessie, poor thing,
Crawls under his wing,
Unable to live on her tod.

Now her life is all torment and lies:
"I crave liberation!" she cries,
And stabs him (it's messy),
But justice gets Tessie –
She's hanged by the neck till she dies.

RON RUBIN

THE UNRHYMED LIMERICK

There was an old man of Dunoon
Who always ate soup with a fork;
    For he said: "As I eat
Neither fish, fowl nor flesh,
I should finish my dinner too quickly."

There once was an elderly trout
Who fell from a dangerous perch;
She emitted a wail,
And exclaimed: "Bless my soul!
Whatever occasioned my flounder?"

H. G. B. BROWN

There was an unfortunate batsman
Whose mother fell under the roller;
    He cried: "All this grease
    Will ruin the pitch!
Go and fetch me a bucket of sawdust."
R. S. STAINIER

There was a young fellow of Slough
Who thought he was terribly tough;
He was set on one day,
On the banks of Newquay,
Till he shouted: "I've had it – I'm through!"

H. A. C. EVANS

There was a young girl of Kilkee
Who went for a swim in the ocean;
When they said: "Is it hot?"
She replied: "No, it isn't –
I could do with a nice cup of cocoa!"

GERARD BENSON

Naughty Limericks

There was a young lady called Gloria
Who was had by Sir Gerald Du Maurier,
Another six men,
Sir Gerald (again),
And the band at the Waldorf Astoria.

In the Garden of Eden lay Adam
Complacently stroking his madam;
   And loud was his mirth,
   For he knew that on Earth
There were only two balls – and he had 'em!

There was a young fellow from Sparta,
A really magnificent farter;
With the wind from one bean,
He'd fart "God Save The Queen",
And Beethoven's "Moonlight Sonata".

When we went to a bistro in Cannes,
That is, me and my girlfriend Joanne,
   The garçon, the swine,
   Dipped his dick in the wine,
And offered Joanne Coq-au-vin!

From the depths of the crypt at St Giles
Came a scream that resounded for miles;
Said the vicar: "Good gracious!
Has father Ignatius
Forgotten the Bishop has piles!"

Come and see our French goods – you must try 'em;
Ensure they're the right size when you buy 'em:
Strong, smooth and reversible,
The thinnest dispersible –
All unusual shapes, we supply 'em.

With a maiden a chap once begat
Bouncing triplets named Pat, Nat and Tat;
'Twas fun in the breeding,
But hell in the feeding:
As there wasn't a spare tit for Tat!

An old preacher from Idaho Springs
Always talked about God and such things;
But his secret desire
Was a guy in the choir,
With a bottom like jelly on springs.

There was a young man from Australia
Who painted his arse like a dahlia;
The colour was fine,
Likewise the design;
The aroma? Ah, that was a failia.

An Argentine gaucho named Bruno
Once said: "There is one thing I do know:
A woman is fine,
And the sheep are divine,
But a llama is Numero Uno!"

A hot-tempered girl from Caracas
Was wed to a samba-mad jackass;
   When he started to cheat her
   With a dark senorita,
She drop-kicked him in the maracas.

Try our Rubber Girlfriend (air-inflatable),
Perennially young (quite insatiable);
   Our satisfied clients
   From mere midgets to giants,
Say she's incredibly sexy and mate-able.

There is a young lady named Aird
Whose bottom is always kept bared;
   When asked why, she pouts,
   And says the Boy Scouts
All beg her to please Be Prepared.

FOR WIDOWER – Wanted: housekeeper,
Not too bloody refined, a light sleeper;
   When employer's inclined,
   Must be game for a grind,
Pay: generous, mind, but can't keep her.

There was a young fellow named Bliss
Whose sex life was strangely amiss;
    For even with Venus
    His recalcitrant penis
Would seldom do better than t
                h
                i
                s

A fellow with passions quite gingery
Was exploring his young sister's lingerie;
    Then, with giggles of pleasure
    He plundered her treasure –
Adding incest to insult and injury.

There was a young man of Dumfries
Who said to his girl: "you please,
    It would give me great bliss
    If, while playing with this,
You would pay some attention to these."

A voluptuous dancer from Wheeling,
Always danced with such exquisite feeling;
    There was never a sound
    For miles around,
Save for fly-buttons hitting the ceiling.

A mathematician named Hall
Has a hexahedronical ball;
The cube of its weight
Times his pecker, plus eight,
Is his phone number – give him a call!

There was a young lady named Hilda
Who went out with a top body-builder;
He said that he should,
That he could and he would,
And he did – and it pretty near killed her!

A pansy who lived in Khartoum
Took a lesbian up to his room,
But they argued a lot
About who should do what,
And quite how and with what and to whom.

A lass of curvaceous physique
Preferred dresses that made her look chic
But all would agree
That topless to knee
Did little to help her mystique.
DOUGLAS CATLEY

There was a young student named Jones
Who'd reduce any maiden to moans
By his wonderful knowledge
(Acquired in college),
Of nineteen erogenous zones.

His neighbours all looked quite askance a lot
At a passionate fellow called Lancelot;
    Whenever he'd pass
    A presentable lass,
The front of his pants would advance a lot.

An old cop from Death Valley Junction,
Whose organ had long ceased to function,
    Deceived his poor wife
    For the rest of her life
With the dexterous use of his truncheon.

There was a young girl of La Plata
Who was widely renowned as a farter;
    Her deafening reports
    At the Argentine Sports,
Made her much in demand as a starter.

While cruising the cosmos, McCavity
Used language of frightful depravity;
    When asked to desist,
    He replied: "I insist –
Out here there is no need for gravity!"
RON RUBIN

A talented cellist in Rio
Was seducing a lady named Cleo;
    As she lowered her panties,
    She said: *"No andantes –*
I want this *allegro con brio!"*

There was a young lady named Maude,
A sort of society fraud;
In the parlour, 'tis told,
She was distant, quite cold,
But on the verandah, my Gawd!

A notorious harlot named Hearst
In the pleasures of men is well-versed;
    Reads the sign at the head
    Of her well-rumpled bed:
"The customer always comes first".

There was a young fellow named Menzies
Whose kissing sent girls into frenzies;
    But a virgin, one night,
    Crossed her legs in a fright,
And fractured his bi-focal lenzies.

An old archaeologist, Throstle,
Discovered a marvellous fossil;
He knew from its bend
And the knob at the end,
'Twas the peter of Paul the Apostle.

There was a young chap of high station
Who was found by a pious relation
Making love in a ditch
With – I won't say a bitch –
But a lady of scant reputation.

There was a young lady of Louth
Who returned from a trip to the South;
Her father said: "Nelly,
There's more in your belly
Than ever went in by your mouth!"

While Titian was mixing rose madder,
His model reclined on a ladder;
Her position, to Titian,
Suggested coition,
So he shinned up the ladder and had 'er.

God's plan made a hopeful beginning,
But Man spoilt his chances by sinning;
We trust that the story
Will end in great glory,
But, at present, the other side's winning!

My dear, you look simply divine,
And I know that we'll get along fine;
For making ends meet
Will be such a treat,
When one end is yours, and one mine.

They say that our parson's young daughter
Loved sex like no decent girl oughter;
But nothing she did
Stimulated her id
Like the spanking she got when he caught her.

At ninety, my Great Uncle Fred
Took a sexy young slapper to bed;
I'm afraid I can't say
If he had it away,
'Cos it's wrong to speak ill of the dead.

When God made his prototype Man,
He mislaid vital parts of the plan;
And unsightly sections,
Like bums and erections,
He ought to improve when he can.

An old Scottish poet, McAmiter
often bragged of excessive diameter;
Though it wasn't the size
That brought tears to their eyes,
But the rhythm – iambic hexameter.

A sprightly old codger from Goring
Was asked why he'd taken up whoring;
   "It's simple,' he said,
   "My wife is stone dead,
And necrophilia's simply dead boring!"

          There was a young fellow from Kent
            Whose tool was incredibly bent;
              To save himself trouble,
                He put it in double,
            And, instead of coming he went!

A bather whose clothing was strewed
By strong winds that had left her quite nude,
   Saw a chap come along,
   And, unless I am wrong,
You expected this line to be rude.

          There was an old bounder of Wadham
         Who approved of the folk ways of Sodom;
           "For a man might," he said,
             "Have a very poor head,
           But be a fine fellow, at bottom!"

A flighty type, hopeless at tennis,
But at swimming and diving a menace,
Took pains to explain:
"It depends how you train –
I *was* a streetwalker in Venice!"

There was an amazing old wizard
Who got a fierce pain in his gizzard;
So he drank wind and snow,
At some fifty-below,
And farted a fifty-day blizzard!

If intercourse gives you thrombosis,
While incontinence causes neurosis,
I'd prefer to expire
Whilst fulfilling desire,
Than live on in a state of psychosis.

A forward young rascal named Farr
Had a habit of goosing his Ma;
"Go and pester your sister,"
She said, when he kissed her,
"I've enough trouble coping with Pa!"

Every time Lady Lowbodice swoons,
Her plump boobies pop out like balloons;
But her butler stands by
With hauteur in his eye,
And lifts them back in with warm spoons.

There was a young maiden of Joppa
Who came a society cropper;
She went off to Ostend
With a gentleman friend,
And the rest of the story's improper.

A virginal maiden named Kate,
Who necked in the dark with her date;
When asked how she'd fared,
Confessed she was scared,
But otherwise doing first rate!

To Tania the touch of a male meant
An emotional cardiac ailment;
An acuteness of breath
Caused her untimely death
In the course of erotic impalement.

There was a young lady of Maine
Who declared she'd a man on the brain;
But you knew from the view
Of her waist, as it grew,
It was not on her brain he had lain.

A remarkable race are the Persians:
They embrace such peculiar diversions;
    They make love all day,
    In the usual way,
And save, till the nights, their perversions.

An amorous writer of verses
Was especially enamoured of nurses;
    But he found each advance
    In pursuit of romance
Met only with starchy reverses.

There was a young maiden from Multerry
Whose knowledge of life was desultory;
    She explained, like a sage:
    "Adolescence? The stage
Between puberty and – er – adultery!"

A virile young soldier of Palma
Leapt straight into bed with his charmer;
    She, naturally nude,
    Said: "Please, don't think me rude,
But, I do wish you'd take off your armour!"

A surgeon of some imprecision,
Decided on self-circumcision;
A slip of the knife –
"Oh dear," said his wife,
"Our sex life will need some revision."

Chimed a charming young hussy of Padua:
"A peso! Why, sir, what a cadua!"
He said, raising his hat:
"You're not worth even that –
All the same, I am glad to have hadua!"

There was a young lawyer named Rex
Who was sadly deficient in sex:
Arraigned for exposure,
He said, with composure:
"De minimis non curat lex!" *

* The Law is not concerned with trifles

King Richard, in one of his rages,
Forsook his good lady for ages,
And rested in bed
With a good book instead,
Or, preferably, one of the pages.

A.B. HALL

There was an old tart from Kilkenny,
Whose usual charge was a penny;
For half of that sum
You might fondle her bum –
A source of amusement to many!

A lovely young lady named Sally
Stripped off at the Working Men's Palais;
She received wild applause
When she slipped off her drawers,
'Cos the hairs on her head didn't tally!

Widow (conscious that time's on the wing),
Fortyish, but still game for a fling,
Seeks fun-loving male,
Mature, but not stale,
With a view to the usual thing,
S. J. SHARPLESS

According to old Sigmund Freud
Life is seldom so fully enjoyed
As in human coition
(In any position)
With the usual organs employed.

"Given faith," quoth the vicar of Deneham,
"From the lusts of the flesh we might wean 'em;
But the human soul sighs
For a nice pair of thighs,
And a little of what lies between 'em."

An amorous maiden, antique,
Kept a man in her house for a week;
    He entered her door
    With a thunderous roar,
But his exit was marked by a squeak.

There was a young princess, Snow White,
Who awoke with a terrible fright;
    She was frightened and shaken –
    She shouldn't have taken
That Seven-Up last thing at night!
GERARD BENSON

When Lazarus came back from the dead,
He still couldn't function in bed;
    "What good's resurrection
    Without an erection?"
Old Lazarus testily said.

A lady I know, rather merry,
Spilt a whole glass of bubbly perry;
    It made quite a mess
    Down the front of her dress,
But what fun as I searched for her cherry!

Said old Father William: "I'm humble,
And getting too weak for a tumble,
But produce me a blonde,
And I'm still not beyond
An attempt at an interesting fumble."
CONRAD AIKEN

Said Mars when entangled with Venus:
"I feel there is *something* between us,
And the sound in my ears
Of Olympian jeers,
Suggests that the blighters have seen us!"
MARY HOLTBY

On an outing with seventeen Czechs,
The tour-guide provided free sex;
She returned from the jaunt
Feeling, well – slightly gaunt,
But the Czechs were all absolute wrecks.

It seems I impregnated Marge,
So I do rather feel, by and large,
Some dough should be tendered
For services rendered,
But I can't decide quite *what* to charge.

A young choral scholar at Kings
Looked just like a cherub, sans wings;
But he had a proclivity
For amorous activity,
And other un-angelic things.

Said a diffident lady named Drood,
The first time she observed a chap nude:
"I'm glad I'm the sex
That's concave, not convex –
For I don't fancy things that protrude!"

"I'm glad pigs can't fly," said young Sellers
(He's one of those worrying fellers);
"For, if they could fly,
They'd shit in the sky,
And we'd all have to carry umbrellas."
RON RUBIN

A Southern hillbilly named Hollis
Used possums and snakes as his solace;
His offspring had scales,
And prehensile tails,
And voted for Governor Wallace.

A giddy young girl up at Girton,
When found out of bounds with no skirt on,
Explained to her tutor:
"I thought it looked cuter –
A subject I'm quite an expert on!"

I, Caesar, when I learned of the fame
Of Cleopatra, I straightway laid claim;
Ahead of my legions
I invaded her regions –
I saw, I conquered, I came!

A lady, an expert on skis,
Went out with a man who said: "Please,
On the next precipice,
Will you give me a kiss?"
She said: "Quick, before somebody sees!"

A young electrician from Distance
Said: "Ma'am, can I be of assistance?"
But he got quite a shock
When she took off her frock,
And said: "Will you test my resistance?"
CYRIL BIBBY

There was a young girl named Bianca
Who retired while the ship was at anchor;
    But awoke, with dismay,
    When she heard the Mate say:
"We must pull up the top sheet and spanker."

There was a young girl from Fort Kent
Who said that she knew what it meant
    When men asked her to dine,
    Gave her chocolates and wine –
She knew what it meant, but she went!

The new cinematic emporium
Is not just a super-sensorium,
    But a highly effectual
    Heterosexual
Mutual masturbatorium.

A lock-keeper's lass in Upavon
Had locks that were black as a raven;
    On her head they were straight,
    But they curled at the gate
Which led to her innermost haven.

CYRIL BIBBY

A wartime young lady of fashion,
Much noted for wit and for passion,
Is known to have said,
As she jumped into bed:
"Here's one thing those bastards won't ration!"

Said a languorous lady called Wade,
On a beach, with her charms all displayed:
"It's so hot in the sun,
Perhaps sex would be fun,
At least that would give me some shade!"

There was a young lady of Slough
Who said that she didn't know how;
Till a young bounder caught her,
And jolly well taught her –
She's lodging in Pimlico now!

Two middle-aged ladies from Fordham
Went out for a walk and it bored 'em;
As they made their way back,
A sex maniac
Leapt out of some trees and ignored 'em.

I still nurture my 48D
And appear in the *Sun*, on page three:
I'll be tickled to bits
That lads ogle my tits –
Sounds like naked ambition to me!
REG LYNES

As the elevator car left our floor,
Poor old Sue caught her boobs in the door;
She yelled a great deal,
But had they been real,
She'd have bellowed considerably more.

"On the beach," said John sadly, '"there's such
A thing as revealing too much"
So he closed both his eyes
At the ranks of bare thighs,
And felt his way through them by touch.
ISAAC ASIMOV

Though his plan, when he gave her a buzz,
Was to do what he normally does,
She declared: "I'm a soul,
Not a sexual goal."
So he shrugged, and called someone who wuss.

A rapscallion, far gone in treachery,
Lured maids to their doom with his lechery;
He invited them in
For the purpose of sin,
Though he said 'twas to look at his etchery.

The enjoyment of sex, although great,
Is in later years said to abate;
This may well be so,
But how would *I* know?
I'm only a hundred-and-eight!

There was a young man of Wood's Hole
Who had an affair with a mole;
A bit of a nancy,
He did like to fancy
Himself in the dominant role.

Said Queen Isabella of Spain:
"I do like it now and again;
But I wish to explain
That by 'now and again"
I mean *now*, and again and again!'

A businesslike harlot from Draper
Once tried an unusual caper;
What made it so nice
Was, you got it half-price
By producing her ad from the paper.

Said the newlyweds staying near Kitely:
"We turn out the electric light nightly;
    It's best to embark
    Upon sex in the dark –
The look of the thing's so unsightly!"

A girl who was touring Zambesi
Said: "Attracting the men is so easy;
    I don't wear any pants,
    And, at every chance,
I stand where it's frightfully breezy."

There was a young man of Belgrade
Who planned to seduce a fair maid,
    And as it befell,
    He succeeded quite well,
And the maid, like the plan, was well laid.
ISAAC ASIMOV

A senorita who strolled on the Corso
Displayed quite a lot of her torso;
    A crowd soon collected,
    And no one objected,
Though some were in favour of more so.

On the boobs of a barmaid in Sale
Are tattooed all the prices of ale;
And on her behind,
For the sake of the blind,
Is the same list of prices in Braille.

A lonely old maid named Loretta
Sent herself an anonymous letter,
Quoting Ellis on sex,
And *Oedipus Rex*,
And exclaimed: "I already feel better!"

When he ravished a maid on a train,
They arrested a bounder called Blaine;
But the ex-virgin cried:
"That's for me to decide,
And I'll be the *last* to complain!"

There was a young fellow called Crouch
Who was courting his lass on the couch;
She said: "Why not a sofa?"
And he exclaimed: "Oh, for
Goodness sake do shut up while I – ouch!"

Undressing a maiden called Sue,
Her seducer remarked: "If it's true
That a nipple a day
Keeps the doctor away,
Think how healthy you must be with two!"

You'll never know how good you are
Till you try to make love in a car;
    Many men meet defeat
    On a darkened back seat,
And it's only the top shots break par.

An innocent bride from the Mission
Remarked, on her first night's coition:
"What an intimate section
To use for connection,
And, Lord! What a silly position!"

An ingenious maid from Vancouver
Won her man with this adroit manoeuvre:
    She jumped on his knee
    With a cry of great glee,
And now nothing on earth will remove her.

A yogi from far-off Beirut,
For women did not care a hoot;
    But his organ would stand
    In a manner quite grand
When a snake-charmer tooted his flute.

A man in a bus queue in Stoke
Unzippered his flies for a joke;
    An old chap gave a shout,
    And almost passed out,
And a lady, nearby, had a stroke!

The unfortunate Dean of South Herts
Was caught importuning some tarts;
    His good wife was shocked
    When the Dean was unfrocked —
For the first time she saw all his parts.

There was a young lady of Norwood
Whose ways were provokingly forward;
    Said her mother: "My dear,
    You wiggle, I fear,
Your posterior just like a whore would!"

A blonde woodwind player named June
Arrived at rehearsals too soon;
    So a man in the band
    Put his flute in her hand,
And it changed to a contra bassoon.

A Boy Scout was having his fill
Of a nice little Brownie near Rhyl;
"We must Be Prepared!"
Said Patrol Leader Aird,
"So these girls are all taking the pill!"

There was a young trollop from Kent
Who claimed not to know what they meant;
When a man asked her age,
She'd reply, in a rage:
"My age is the age of consent!"

Some gels, and I don't understand 'em
Will strip off their clothing at random,
Without any qualms,
To exhibit their charms –
In short: *quod erat demonstrandum!*

There was a fair lady from Bangor
Who drove young men frantic with anger
By going to matins
In see-through white satins,
Till the vicar was forced to harangue her.

I heard of a story so fraught
With disaster, of balls that got caught,
 When a chap took a crap
 In the woods, and a trap
Underneath… oh, I can't bear the thought!

There's an ointment that makes willies bigger.
It's a fact, be more tactful, don't snigger;
 You'll be hung like a horse,
 Not a real one, of course,
But a fair match for Roy Rogers' Trigger!

There was a young lady called Ransom
Who was serviced four times in a Hansom;
 When she cried: "Give me more!"
 A weak voice from the floor
Protested: "It's Simpson, not Samson!"

A handsome young laundress called Spangle
Had tits tilting up at an angle;
 "They may tickle my chin,"
 She confessed, with a grin,
 "But at least they stay clear of the mangle!"

Along windy rivers in Hunts,
Young couples make love in their punts;
Beneath weeping willows,
They lie on their pillows
And murmur their gratified grunts.

An unusual lady named Grace
Had her eyes in a very strange place;
She could sit on the hole
Of a mouse or a mole,
And stare the poor beast in the face!

There was an old maid from Bermuda
Who shot a marauding intruder;
    It wasn't her ire
    At his lack of attire,
But he reached for her jewels as he screwed her.

A young Spaniard who's hung like a horse
Is first choice with the ladies, of course;
    They long for a dong
    That can bong a huge gong –
So this Juan is their primary source.

A bit of a wanker named Willy
Was informed masturbation is silly:
    "You will probably find
    It will make you go blind!"
But he fondles his dick willy-nilly.

A naturist rambler named Ron
Walks in nothing but boots and a thong;
    Over stiles, arse in air,
    Is apparently where
The remark "Hello, cheeky!" comes from.

Prince Charming was worried to bits –
All the girls in the town had nice tits,
But no *nether* part
Had captured his heart,
Till he cried out: "Oh, Cinders, it fits!"

Ex-telephonist Gladys I'm told
(Now a tart with a heart of pure gold),
Sympathizes with tricks
Minus lead in their dicks,
And quite happily puts them on "hold".

A painter from outside Red Bluff
Hired a model to pose in the buff;
She had such a huge ass,
He discovered, alas,
That his canvas was not big enough!

A young lady whose breasts were quite wee,
Little more than the stings of a bee,
Decided implants
Were the way to enhance
What's become a huge 42 (Gee!)

A golfer who drives with some force,
Played a round at a Nudist Camp Course;
On losing control
Of his shot he was told:
"It's goodbye to one's balls in this gorse!"

A gorilla that lives in the Zoo
Gets bored with so little to do,
He waves his long dong,
And hoses the throng –
Watch out! Next time it might be you.

A barrel of lard known as Lyn
Realized that he'd never be thin;
He weighed half a ton,
Not including his bum,
And God *knows* when he'd last seen his thing!

A bat and a bat in a cave
Were wondering which one was Dave;
It's hard, in the dark,
To tell them apart,
But the bat with the balls must be fave.

"Now really, young man, you're a bore,"
Said Lady Priscilla Flax-Gore,
    "You are covered in sweat,
    And you haven't come yet,
And my God! It's a quarter past four!"

An ample young lady of Eton,
Whose figure had plenty of meat on;
    Said: "Marry me, dear,
    And you'll find that my rear
Is a nice place to warm your cold feet on!"

A confident maiden named Etta
Preferred to be clad in a sweater;
    Three reasons she had:
    Keeping warm was not bad,
But the other two reasons were better.

A sensible sailor named Wyatt
Kept a sizeable whore on the quiet;
    And down by the wharf
    He kept also a dwarf,
In case he should go on a diet.

There's an over-sexed lady called White
Who insists on a dozen per night;
A fellow named Cheddar
Had the brashness to wed her –
His chance of survival is slight.

A wanton young maiden of Wimley,
Reproached for not acting more primly,
Answered: "Heavens above!
I know sex isn't love,
But it's such an attractive facsimile!"

There was a young fellow named Willy
Who acted remarkable silly:
At an All-Nations Ball,
Dressed in nothing at all,
He claimed that his costume was Chile!

Said Miss Farrow, on one of her larks:
"Sex is more fun in bed than in parks;
You feel more at ease,
Your ass doesn't freeze,
And passers-by don't make remarks."

To her gardener, a lady named Lilliom,
Said: "Billy, plant roses and trilium."
   Then she started to fool
   With the gardener's tool,
And wound up in the bed of Sweet William.

After lunch the old Duchess of Beck
Announced: "f you'll listen one sec,
   We've found a chap's tool
   In the main swimming pool,
So – would all of you gentlemen check?"

As dull as the life of the cloister
(Except it's a little bit moister)
   Mutatis mutandum
   Non est disputandum –
There's no thrill in sex for the oyster.

A sturdy young fellow from Poole
Was blessed with a ruddy great tool;
   When fully extended
   The bloody thing ended
A couple of miles short of Goole!

Concerning the bees and the flowers
In the fields and the gardens and bowers,
You will note at a glance
That their ways of romance
Haven't any resemblance to ours.

There was a young girl whose frigidity
Approached cataleptic rigidity,
Till you plied her with drink,
When she'd soon enough sink
To a state of compliant liquidity.

There was a young lady named Lynne
So immersed in original sin,
When they said: "Do be good!
She said: "would if I could!"
And went (straightaway) at it again.

There once was a lady named Mabel,
Always ready, and willing, and able;
And so full of spice,
She could name her own price –
Look at Mabel, all wrapped up in sable!

A disgusting young man named McGill
Made his neighbours exceedingly ill,
    When they learned of his habits
    Involving tame rabbits,
And a bird with a flexible bill!

A lady, removing her scanties,
Heard them crackle electrical shanties;
    Said her husband: "My dear,
    I very much fear
You are suffering amps in your panties!"

There once was a maiden of Siam
Who said to her young sweetheart, Kiam:
    "If you take me, of course,
    You must do it by force –
For God knows you are stronger than I am!"

A gentle old lady I knew
Was dozing one day in her pew;
    When the Preacher yelled: "Sin!'
    She said: "Yo! Count me in!
As soon as the service is through!"

"I admit I'm a bit of a tart,"
Says a Hollywood actress with heart,
"That's why what I need
Is a masculine lead
Who'll allow me to build up his part!"
REG LYNES

There was a young boy, Jack Horner,
Who played with his plums in a corner;
    Said his father: "That's bad,
    When I was a lad,
I preferred a massage down the sauna."
FIONA PITT-KETHLEY

A round-bottomed gal from Mobile
Longed for years to be screwed by a seal;
    But down at the Zoo,
    They declared: "No can do!"
Though the seal was hot for the deal.

A naïve young lady of Cork
Was told she was brought by the stork;
    But after a day,
    With a gent called O'Shea,
She was wary of that kind of talk.
REG YEARLEY

A naked young tart named Roselle
Promenaded the streets with a bell;
When asked why she rang it,
She answered: "God, dang it!
Can't you *see* I've got something to sell!"

A prostitute living in London
Went pantless, with zippers all undone;
She'd explain; "Well, you see,
I can do two or three,
While Ruby next door's getting one done."
DOUGLAS CATLEY

There was a young lady of Brabant
Who slept with an impotent savant;
She admitted: "We shouldn't,
But it turned out he couldn't,
So you can't say we have when we haven't!"

There was a young fellow called Shit,
A name he disliked quite a bit;
So he changed it to Shite –
A step in the right
Direction, one has to admit,
VICTOR GRAY

There was a young man from New York
Whose morals were lighter than cork;
"Young chicks," stated he,
"Hold no terrors for me:
The bird I fear most is the stork!"

A mortician who practised in Fyfe,
Made love to the corpse of his wife;
   "I couldn't know, Judge;
    She was cold, didn't budge –
The same as she acted in life."

Said a chap of his wee Morris Minor:
"For petting, it couldn't be finer;
But for love's consummation,
A wagon called station
Would offer a playground diviner!"

A young motorcyclist from Horton
Whose cock's a particularly short 'un,
   Makes up for the loss
   With the balls of a hoss,
And the stroke of a 500 Norton.

An ugly old harlot called Gert
Used to streetwalk until her corns hurt;
But these days she stands
Upside down on her hands,
With her face covered up by her skirt.

A precocious young lady named Hall
Once attended a birth-control ball;
　　She was loaded with pessaries,
　　And other accessories –
But no-one approached her at all.

An amorous lassie named Harriet
Took on two willing lads in a chariot,
　　Then six monks and ten tailors,
　　Nine priests and six sailors,
Mohammed and Judas Escariot!

Three lovely young girls from St Thomas,
Frequented dance-halls in pyjamas;
　　Being fondled all summer
　　By bass, sax and drummer –
It's a miracle they're not all mammas!

The delightful bartender at Sweeney's
Is renowned for his cocktails and wienies;
　　But I thought him uncouth
　　To gulp gin and vermouth,
Chill the glasses, and piddle martinis!

A Victorian gent said: "This dance,
The Can-Can, which we've got from France,
Fills me with disgust,
It generates lust –
You should see it while you have the chance!"
FRANK RICHARDS

Two she-camels spied on a goat:
One jealously said: "You will note
She leaves the Sheik's tent
With her tail oddly bent,
And clumps of fur pulled from her coat!"

To his bride said a duffer named Clarence:
"I trust you will show some forebearance;
My sexual habits
I picked up from rabbits,
And occasionally watching my parents."

An industrious young obstetrician
Conceived his financial position
To depend upon beauty
And husbandly duty,
And determined and endless coition.

There was a young lady called Burton
Who outraged other fellows at Girton,
By cycling to town
Without wearing a gown,
And, what's more, without even a skirt on!

There was a young lady of Nantes
Who was *très jolie et piquante;*
But her thing was so small
It was no use at all,
Except for *la plume de ma tante.*

A damsel, seductive and handsome,
Got wedged in a sleeping-car transom;
When she offered much gold
For release, she was told
That the view was worth more than the ransom.

Said the Duchess of Chester, at tea:
"Now, young man, do you fart when you pee?'
I replied, with quick wit:
"Do you belch when you shit?"
She conceded. One-nothing to me!

A painter of Pop Art named Jacques,
Decorated each canvas to shock;
Outsize genitalia
Gave viewers heart failure,
But the critics just sneered: "Poppycock!"

A chap with venereal fear
Had intercourse in his wife's ear;
Said she: "I don't mind,
Except that I find
When the telephone rings, I don't hear!"

A pretty young maiden named Flo
Said: "I hate to be had in the snow.
While I'm normally hot,
In this spot I am not –
So, as soon as you come Bert, let's go!"

Said a certain old Earl that I knew:
"I've been struck from the rolls of *Who's Who*,
Just because I was found
Cavorting around
With a housemaid, and very nice too!"

The typists at Wheesley and Beasley
All fornicate freely and easily;
   And in this pleasant way,
   They can top up their pay,
Which at Wheesley and Beasley is measley.

              A certain young girl from Key West
              Was unusually large in the chest;
                  Her boyfriend's attention
                  To her ample dimension
            Brought his own measurement to its best.

To his wife said Sir Hubert le Dawes:
"Fix this chastity belt to your drawers!"
   But an amorous Celt
   Found the key to the belt,
While the squire was away at the wars.

Said the crafty old Doctor McSommon:
"Impotence is becoming too common:
   Pills, oysters and honey?
   A complete waste of money –
What works every time's a hot woman!"

Whenever I wear winklepickers,
The footsteps behind are the vicar's;
It's the backs of my shoes
He likes to peruse –
Or perhaps it's the cut of my knickers!

A short-sighted actor, enraged,
Muttered thus to an actress on stage:
"When I fell for you,
I believed fifty-two
Was the size of your tits, not your age!"

Softly seductive, sweet Brenda
Wants a chap who is charming and tender,
And thoughtful, and bright,
And sexually right,
But mostly a very big spender!

There is a young maid in Kilkenny
Who is bothered by lovers so many,
That the saucy young elf
Means to raffle herself,
And the tickets are two for a penny!

There was a old guy from Lone Pine
Who lived with three wives at a time;
When asked: "Why the third?"
He replied: "One's absurd,
And bigamy, sir, is a crime!"

There was a young lady named Hopper
Who became a society cropper;
She determined to go
To Bordeaux with her beau…
And the rest of the story's improper.

There was a young lady called Claire
Who streaked in the park for a dare;
And all those who saw
Could not agree more:
She had a magnificent pair!

There was a young girl from Penzance
Who had clearly forgotten her pants
Under such a thin dress
(off-the-peg, M&S) – ,
That's why all the lads asked her to dance.

There was a young lady called Tess
Who went to a Ball, in a dress;
   But the cut was so low
   That her boobs were on show –
I did have a quick look, I confess!

There once was a handsome young sheikh,
With a marvellous penile physique;
   Though its length and its weight
   Made it look really great,
He fell woefully short on technique.

A bikini-clad lady in Bude
Wondered: 'Why are the men quite so rude?
   When I bathe in the sea,
   They will all follow me
In the hope that my boobs will protrude!

Said the Duke to the Duchess of Avery,
With abandon that teetered on bravery:
   "You've been sitting on *Punch*
   Since, oh – long before lunch –
Might I have it before it's unsavoury?"

An apparently shy girl of Pecking
Would indulge in a great deal of necking;
    Which seemed such a waste,
    Since she claimed to be chaste –
This last statement, however, needs checking.

What he asked for (a four-letter word)
Badly frightened the virgin Miss Byrd;
    London Gin and insistence
    Wore down her resistance –
The four-letter word then occurred.

There was a young lady of Chester
Who fell madly in love with a jester;
    Though her breath came out hotly
    At the sight of his motley,
It was really his wand that impressed her!

Said a chic and attractive young Greek:
"Would you like a quick peek that's unique?"
    "Why, yes," he confessed,
    So she quickly undressed,
And showed him her sleek Greek physique!

"Said a voice from the back of the car:
Young man, I don't know who you are,
    But allow me to state,
    Though it may be too late:
I had not meant to come quite this far!"

An aristocratic old Count
Who fell madly in love with his mount,
    Said: "My status enables
    Behaviour in stables
For which I'm not *bound* to account!"
REG LYNES

Well, you may be a famous MP,
But you're not all you're cracked up to be;
    I just can't remember
    When your standing member
Last lost its deposit in me!

There was an old monk in Siberia
Whose resistence grew steadily wearier,
    Till he burst from his cell,
    With a hell of a yell,
And eloped with the Mother Superior.

In the shade of a palm tree at Sousse,
He said: "*J'aime tes deux pamplemousses.*"
With languorous sigh
She murmured reply:
"*Je pense que ta banana est douche.*"

There was a young lady named Claire
Who possessed a magnificent pair;
Or that's what I thought,
Till I saw one get caught
On a thorn, and begin to lose air!

There are several good reasons why Walter
Is determined that he'll never alter:
Afternoons that he spends
With unusual friends,
And weekends clad in saddle and halter.
REG LYNES

A girl who went in for a swim
In the nude, said "It's great once you're in."
The chap with the cock
Who gave her such a shock,
Said it certainly felt great to him!

Naughtier
Limericks

I can't see the hole

A young lady golfer named Duff
Had a lovely, luxuriant muff;
In his haste to get in her,
One eager beginner
Lost both of his balls in the rough.

No wonder young maidens would cower
At the thought of bold Owen Glendower:
They say he had balls
Like the dome of St Paul's,
And a prick like the Post Office Tower.

Pray tell me, dear, who is that chump
Who stands there, all naked and plump,
    With his tool in his ear,
    Appearing, from here,
Like a rather obscene petrol pump?

There was a young girl of Baroda
Who built an erotic pagoda;
The walls of its halls
Were festooned with the balls
And the tools of the fools who bestrode her.

I met a lewd nude in Bermuda,
Who thought she was shrewd, I was shrewder;
    She considered it crude
    To be wooed in the nude –
I pursued her, subdued her, and screwed her.

There was a young cad from Belgrave
Who kept a dead whore in a cave;
    He said: 'I admit
    I'm a bit of a shit –
But think of the money I'll save!'

There was a young fellow named Cass
Whose bollocks were made out of brass;
When they tinkled together,
They played "Stormy Weather",
And lightening shot out of his ass!

Fitzpatrick, Fitzgerald and me
Are frightfully gay company;
Fitz P fits Fitz G,
And Fitz G fits Fitz P,
And each of those Fitzes fits me!

There was an old man of Dundee
Who molested an ape in a tree;
The result was most horrid –
All arse and no forehead,
Three balls and a purple goatee.

A young maiden of English nativity
Had a fanny of rare sensitivity;
She could sit on the lap
Of a Nazi or Jap,
And detect his Fifth Column activity.

There was a young virgin named Jeanie
Whose dad was a terrible meanie:
He fashioned a hatch
With a latch for her snatch –
She could only be had by Houdini.

A student who hailed from St John's
Badly wanted to bugger the swans;
"Oh, no!" said a porter,
"Please, bugger my daughter –
Them swans is reserved for the dons!"

A keen lassie who has to have cock
Every hour, on the hour, round the clock,
Cries: "Two, four, six, eight –
Times three. I can't wait!"
And she keeps a spare tucked in her frock.

A Hollywood star named De Niro
Who had never been cast as a hero,
Decided to start
To build up his part –
Now a porn star, his cock weighs a kilo!

"It has been such a marvellous day,"
Yawned Her Ladyship Dougal MacKay:
"Three blackberry tarts,
At least forty farts,
Two shits and a bloody good lay!"

A Salvation Army lass, Claire,
Was having her first love affair;
    As she climbed into bed,
    She reverently said:
"I wish to be opened by prayer."

Well buggered's a chap called Delpasse
By the rest of the lads in his class;
    He insists, with a yawn:
    "Now the novelty's gone,
This is simply a pain in the ass!"

A facetious old Don of Divinity
Boasted loudly his daughter's virginity:
    "They must have been dawdling
    Down at old Magdalen –
It wouldn't have happened at Trinity!"

There was a young lady of Exeter,
So pretty that men craned their necks at her;
    And one was so brave
    As to take out and wave
The distinguishing sign of his sex at her.

There was a young lady named Eva
Who filled up her bath to receive her;
She took off her clothes,
From her head to her toes,
And a voice through the keyhole yelled: "Beaver!"

A friend has an end to his member
That, once seen, one would always remember;
The size of this knob's
Too big for most gobs,
So cock-sucking's off the agenda!

"Give me cock, give me cock, give me cock!"
Chants a chick with a mantra to shock;
There is nothing this hippie
Likes more than a quickie,
And the queue stretches right round the block

Said the Queen to the King: "I don't frown on
The fact that you choose to go down on
    My page on the stairs,
    But you'll give the boy airs,
If you *will* do the job with your crown on."

Said Nelson at his most la-di-da-di:
"I am sorry if I'm rather tardy,
    But I'm in a dilemma –
    Should I bugger Emma,
Or screw the delectable Hardy?"
A. CINNA

A young man by his girl was desired
To give her the thrills she required;
    But he died of old age
    Ere his cock could assuage
The volcanic desires it inspired.

There was an old fellow in Ewing,
Whose poor heart stopped while he was screwing;
    He gasped: "Really, Miss,
    Don't feel bad about this –
There is nothing I'd rather die doing!"
Said Old Father William: "I'm humble,

And getting too old for a tumble,
    But produce me a blonde,
    And I'm still not beyond
An attempt at an interesting fumble."
CONRAD AIKEN

                    An old man from Cattahoochee
                    Arrived home as drunk as can be;
                    He wound up the clock
                    With the end of his cock,
                    And buggered his wife with the key.

A whore for a bit of a joke,
Wears an invisibility cloak;
    Tricks can't tell if they're fucking
    Or sucking or mucking
About with a bird or a bloke!

The French are a race among races –
They will screw in the funniest places;
    Any orifice handy
    Is considered quite dandy,
And that goes for the one in their faces.

A well-endowed chap with a cock

Several sizes too big for his jock,
    Eventually found
    It was far better wound
Round one leg, and tucked into his sock!

"Active balls?" said an old chap of Stoneham,
    "I regret that I no longer own 'em.
        But I hasten to say
        They were good in their day –
    De mortuis nil nisi bonum."

C. D. CUDMORE

There's a very prim girl called McDrood:
What a combo – both nympho and prude!
    She wears her dark glasses
    When fellows make passes,
And keeps her eyes shut when she's screwed.

There was a young girl from Pitlochry,
Who was had by a man in the rockery,
    She said: "Oh you've come,
     All over my bum –
This isn't a fuck it's a mockery!"

There was a young fellow called Chubb
Who joined a smart buggery club;
    But his parts were so small,
    He was no use at all,
And they promptly refunded his sub.

We sailed on the good ship Venus,
By God, you should have seen us;
    The figure-head
    Was a whore in bed –
Sucking a dead man's penis.

There once was a sinister Ottoman,
To the fair sex I fear he was not a man;
    He evaded the charms
    Of feminine arms –
"Quite frankly," he said "I'm a bottom man!"

A fellow who fucks but as few can,
Had a fancy to try with a toucan;
　　He admits, like a man,
　　The collapse of his plan:
"I can't – but I bet none of you can!"

An ingenious bod called Racine
Has invented a fucking machine;
　　Concave or convex,
　　It will suit either sex –
With attachments for those in between.

When a horny young curate from Leeds
Was discovered one day in the weeds
   Astride a young nun,
   He cried: "This is fun!
Far better than telling one's beads!"

There was a young stud from Missouri
Who screwed with astonishing fury,
   Till taken to court
   For his vigorous sport,
And condemned by a poorly hung jury.

An enormously fat girl, Regina,
Employed a young water diviner
   To play a slick trick,
   With his prick as a stick,
To help relocate her vagina.

"I cannot be bothered with drawers,"
Insists one of our better-known whores;
   "There isn't much doubt
   I do better without
In conducting my everyday chores."

A taxi-cab whore out of Iver,
Would do the round trip for a fiver;
    Quite reasonable too,
    For a sightsee, a screw,
And a fifty pence tip for the driver.
VICTOR GRAY

There was an old madam called Rainey,
Adept at her business, and brainy;
    She charged forty bucks for
    An experienced whore,
And a five-dollar bill for a trainee.

Of my husband I do not ask much,
Just an all mod and con little hutch;
    Bank account in my name,
    With the cheque book the same,
Plus a small fee for fucking and such.

The orgy began on the lawn,
Several hours ahead of the dawn;
    We found ourselves viewing
    Sixty-six couples screwing,
But by sun-up they'd all come, and gone!

A bashful young fellow of Brighton
Would never make love with the light on;
    His girlfriend said: "Noel!
    You're in the wrong hole –
There's plenty of room in the right 'un!"
E.O. PARROTT

There was a young Turkish cadet,
And this is the damndest one yet –
    His tool was so long
    And incredibly strong,
He could bugger six Greeks *en brochette*!

A harlot from Kalamazoo
Filled up her vagina with glue;
    And said, with a grin:
    "If they pay to get in,
They can pay to get out again too!"

A price-concious hooker called Annie,
Whose tariff was cheap but quite canny,
    Charged a pound for a fuck,
    Fifty pence for a suck,
And two bob for a feel of her fanny.

There was a young lady from Natchez
Who was fully equipped with two snatches;
She often cried: "Shit!
I'd give either tit
For a chap with equipment that matches!"

The vicar of Dunstan St Just,
All consumed with a bestial lust,
Raped the Bishop's prize owls,
Fucked a few startled fowls,
And buggered a buzzard that bust!

There was a young lady from Brussels
Whose pride was her vaginal muscles;
She could easily flex them,
And so interflex them
As to whistle love songs through her bustles.

There was a young girl from Aberystwyth
Who took grain to the mill to make grist with;
The miller's son, Jack,
Laid her on her back,
And united the organs they pissed with.
ALGERNON CHARLES SWINBURNE

A platinum-blonde, Goldilocks,
Who kept a *ménage* near the docks,
Had it off with three bears
Near Wapping Old Stairs,
And infected them all with the pox.
FIONA PITT-KETHLEY

Come to Nora's for wine and strong waters,
And for diddling in clean, classy quarters;
　　I assure every guest
　　I've made personal test
Of my booze, and my beds, and my daughters!

There was a young lady of Ealing,
And her lover before her was kneeling;
　　She said: "Dearest Jim,
　　Take your hand from my quim –
I much prefer fucking to feeling!"
ISAAC ASIMOV

There was an old fellow called Ziegel
Who decided he'd bugger a beagle;
But just as he came,
A voice called his name,
Saying: "Naughty! You know it's illegal."

An experienced hooker, Arlene,
Said: "Give me a lad of eighteen;
　　His pecker gets harder,
　　There's more cream in his larder,
And he fucks with a vigour obscene!"

A classical chap from Victoria,
In a post-alcoholic euphoria,
   Was discovered one day
   In a club for the gay,
Immersed in an *ars amatoria*.

There was a young student at Queens
Who haunted the public latrines;
   He was heard, in the john,
   Shouting: "Bring me a don!
But, please, spare me those dreary old Deans."

A geneticist living in Rheims,
In attempting to learn what life means,
   Has discovered the zip
   On a sizeable dick,
And insists that it's all in the jeans!

A young lass with a prize-winning bum
Entertained all the lads, one by one,
   Till a bugger from Dover
   Said: "Why not turn over –
And we can have *twice* as much fun!"

There was a young man from East Anstey
Who suggested to his girlfriend, Nancy:
    "Straightforward or oral,
    Or backwards, or whoral?
I'm game for what tickles your fancy!"

An old lighthouse-keeper from Orme
Snuggled up to his wife to keep warm;
    She said: "Darling, your cock
    Is like Eddystone Rock,
In its shape and in colour and form!"

A Scots sailor christened McPhie,
Spoonerizes embarrassingly;
    He once shouted: "You wanker!"
    Instead of: "Weigh anchor!"
And introduces himself as 'PhcMie'.

What is pinkish and roundish and hairy,
And hangs from a bush, light and airy,
    Much hidden away
    From the broad light of day,
Beneath a stiff prick? A gooseberry!

A coroner reported, in Preston:
"The verdict is anal congestion;
   I found an eight-ball,
   And a sailmaker's awl
Halfway up the commander's intestine!"

A cheerful young golfer named Jock
Gave his shot a three-hundred-yard sock;
   It doesn't sound far
   For a man who shoots par,
But 'twas done with the end of his cock!

I know a young man in Calcutta
Who plasters his member with butter,
   Then lovingly screws
   A sack of cashews –
He must be a right fucking nutter!

There was a young girl from Detroit
Who, at fucking, was very adroit:
   She'd contract her vagina
   To a pinpoint, or finer,
Or widen it out, like a quoit.

Bibliography

There are numerous books of entertaining limericks which are well worth reading.

Here is a small selection:
Out On A Limerick Bennett, Cerf (Cassell & Co. Ltd), 1961
The Art of The Limerick, Cyril Bibby
(The Research Publishing Co.), 1978
Loopy Limericks, Picked by John Foster (Collins), 2001
The Oxford Book of Comic Verse, Edited by John Gross
(OUP), 1995
The Complete Limerick Book, Langford Reed (Jarrolds), 1924
1001 Limericks, Selected by M Clapham & R Gray (Book
Blocks/CRW Publishing Ltd), 2003
The Penguin Book of Limericks, Compiled and edited by
E. O. Parrott (Penguin Books Ltd), 1983
Limericks, Michael Palin (Hutchinson), 1985
The Blue Peter Book of Limericks, Edited by Biddy Baxter &
Rosemary Gill (Pan Books/BBC), 1972
Very Rude Limericks Stephen Cordwell, (Grange Books), 1996
Mr Punch's Limerick Book, Edited by Langford Reed
(Cobden-Sanderson), 1934
The Looniest Limerick Book in the World, Joseph Rosenbloom
(Sterling Publishing Co.), 1982
1000 Limericks for Kids, Joel Rothman (Ward Lock), 1985
I'm Sorry I Haven't A Clue, Compiled by Jon Naismith
(Orion Media), 1998
Limerick Delight, Chosen, by E. O. Parrott (Puffin Books), 1985
The Armada Book of Limericks, Compiled by Mary Danby
(Fontana Paperbacks), 1977
The Second Armada Book of Limericks, Compiled by Mary Danby
(Fontana Paperbacks), 1978
Loads and Loads of Limericks, Collected by David G. Harris

The 101 Best and Only Limericks of Spike Milligan, Spike Milligan
(Hobbs/Michael Joseph), 1982

Limeroons, Noel Ford (Puffin), 1991

Spooky Rhymes, Willis Hall (Hamlyn/Egmont)

Lecherous Limericks, Isaac Asimov (Panther Books)

Lickerish Limericks, Cyril Ray (JM Dent & Sons Ltd), 1979

Explosion of Limericks, Vivian Holland (Cassell)

The Tiny Book of Dirty Limericks, (Harper Collins), 2002

The Wordsworth Book of Limericks, Edited by Linda Marsh
(Wordsworth Editions), 1997

More of The World's Best Dirty Limericks, Richard O'Toole
(Harpercollins), 1994

Book of American Limericks, Carolyn Wells
(GP Putnams & Sons), 1925

Bawdy Limericks, (Sphere Books), 1987

Lots of Limericks, Louis Untermeyer (W. H. Allen), 1962

The Star Book of Saucy Limericks, (Star/W. H. Allen), 1982

Out On A Limerick Ron Rubin, (New Millenium), 1995

The Little Book of Naughty Limericks, Edited by Tom Keegan
(Parragon),1998

Lancashire Limericks, John Sephton (Landy Publishing)

East Riding Limericks, Compiled by Howard Peach (Hutton Press),
1989

There was a Young Lady from Bude, A Book of West Country
Limericks (Romper Bude), 1987

Great Green Limericks, Selected from the *Observer* Great Green
Limerick Competition run in association with Friends of The Earth
(A Star Book/W. H. Allen & Co), 1989

The Bunbury Book of Limericks, The Reverend Septimus Bunbury
(Queen Anne Press), 1988

The Arrival Press Book of Limericks, Edited by Tim Sharp
(Arrival Press), 1996

Limericks Let Loose, Tom Mohan (Minerva Press), 1999

Limericks For Lunchbreaks, J. Michael Fitzjoseph (Seven Islands Press)

There was an Old Fellow from Tring, Antony Wootten (Electric Monk Publishing), 2000

Limrigau, Edited by Tegwyn Jones (Carreg Gwalch), 2000

Rhymes for an Idle Moment, Tony Channon (Eliton Books), 2002

Odes & Ends, Cyril Fletcher (A Dragon Book), 1982.

Limericks For The Erudite, Warrick Elrod

A person from Britain whose Head was the Shape of a Mitten, N. M. Bodecker (J. M. Dent & Sons Ltd), 1980

Terse Verse, Cyril Fletcher (Book Club Associates)

The Listing Attic, Edward Gorey (Duell, Sloan & Pearce)

Verse Places, John Slim (Underwood Enterprises), 2000

Lewd Limericks, Michael Horgan (Foulsham), 2003

The Limerick, Gershon Legman (Jupiter Books), 1969

Acknowledgments

The editor and publisher are grateful to the following for permission to publish their limericks for the first time in this collection:

JOHN ABERCROMBIE
'In skydiving he found some expression', 'It may be of interest to know', 'The driveway was almost complete', 'Good health is more precious than riches', 'It is sad but it's true that the donkey', 'My absence from bed was recorded', 'As a practising sit-on-the-fencer' and 'In trying to rhyme the word 'orange" copyright © John Abercrombie 2008.

GERARD BENSON
'A rat does not purr like a cat' and 'I've been teaching my poodle to play' copyright © Gerard Benson 2008.

MARGARET BRACE
'Archaeologists dig at their leisure', 'While writing a letter to Ron', 'The discussion became very heated', 'An ambitious couple from Leeds', 'In developing submarine doors', 'There's many a computer geek', 'Said an artist: 'I'll throw a big party", and 'There was a young girl from Caerphilly' copyright © Margaret Brace 2008.

PAT BROCK
'The model, preparing to pose' and 'In Florida, famous for fun' copyright © Pat Brock 2008.

LORRAINE CANNING
'An incautious gourmet called Shaun' copyright © Lorraine Canning 2008.

MICK CARDIFF
'I shall melt in your warm arms,' he told her' and 'There is a young lady from Splott' copyright © Mick Cardiff 2008.

LILIAN CHAVERT
'Said a very plump girl from Devizes' and 'Said a homeless rough-sleeper named Jones' copyright © Lilian Chavert 2008.

CHRISTMAS COLE
'The donkey, a fat, lazy mule' copyright © Christmas Cole 2008.

MARY DANIELS
'A ladybird lost a black spot', 'My rhymes are not bawdy or rude' and 'The Natterjack Toad learned to knit' copyright © Mary Daniels 2008.

DICKIE DUNN
'There was an old Prophet called Jonah' copyright © Dickie Dunn 2008.

ESDON FROST
'An inquisitive student from Dorking', 'There was an old pedant from Shoreham', 'With respect to the great Mr Lear' and 'We're left in a state of near-trauma' copyright © Esdon Frost 2008.

PAM GIDNEY
'A camel with nothing to do', 'I went on a flight out to Tresco', 'I put all my eggs in one basket', 'He muffets his way from the ceiling' and 'My computer has gone on the blink' copyright © Pam Gidney 2008.

EILEEN GILMOUR
'As Noah looked out with a frown', 'As the Spice Girls gyrated on stage' and 'An inspired young writer called Dicky' All copyright © Eileen Gilmour 2008.

CATHERINE GRAHAM
'A musical chap, named McDoon' copyright © Catherine Graham 2008.

DOREEN HANCOX
'Quite the daftest that Nature could pick', 'As it sat on its holly-trimmed plate', 'If she ever gets caught in the rain', 'A gardener who once lived in Harrow', 'A gardener who hailed from Dundee', 'A nurseryman was most unwise', 'An old men's-outfitter named Bert', 'The drinks left for him by each bed' copyright © Doreen Hancox 2008, and reproduced with the kind permission of Bill and Steve Hancox.

DON HENDERSON
'A musical lady named Glenda' copyright © Don Henderson 2008.

IAN HERBERT
'A turkey who lived on a hill', 'An extrovert, yodelling squirrel', 'A diet-concious mountain gorilla', 'A wiry and sinuous eel' and 'A centipede whose full name was Heather' copyright © Ian Herbert 2008.

PAMELA TRUDIE HODGE
'A ghost from a graveyard in Havant' and 'A reluctant Italian grocer' copyright © Pamela Trudie Hodge 2008.

MARY HOLTBY
'There once was a man of Madrid', 'If high for superfluous fat you rate', 'There once was a housewife of Pisa', 'In the works of a woman called Anna', 'A curious beast is the lion' and 'Said she, with a sniff of disgust' copyright © Mary Holtby 2008.

SA HOPKINS
'A young motorcyclist from Horton' copyright © SA Hopkins 2008.

MARY INGHAM
'There was a young dancer called Sally' copyright © Mary Ingham 2008.

MELISSA LAWRENCE
'There was a young lady from Chester', 'There's a gluttonous chap in New York', 'There once was a writer called Reuel' and 'There was a young man from that town in Wales with the really long name' copyright © Melissa Lawrence 2008.

SARAH LINGARD
'A poodle quite desperate to dance' copyright © Sarah Lingard 2008.

GARY LUCAS
'Give me cock, give me cock, give me cock!' copyright © Gary Lucas 2008.

PETER LUCAS
'There was a young man from East Anstey' and 'An old lighthouse-keeper from Orme' copyright © Peter Lucas 2008.

REG LYNES
'The Yankees were playing The Mets', 'The poet was stuck for a rhyme', 'Captain Hook was not pleased with his lot', 'I've eaten as much as I can', 'A mermaid who swims off St Ives', 'Our butcher wastes no scrap of meat', 'There are three sorts of sailors: The Cruisers', 'A poorly Man U fan I know', 'Our keeper weighs four-hundred plus', 'I bowled my best googlie at Gatting', 'A goalkeeper christened 'The Cat' and other limericks copyright © Reg Lynes 2008.

CELINA MACDONALD
'My jumper was smart though not posh' copyright © Celina Macdonald 2008.

ACKNOWLEDGMENTS

VIOLET MACDONALD
'Thr wnce ws a grl frm SX' copyright © Violet Macdonald 2008.

CHARLOTTE McBEE
'An inflexible hunter named Potter', 'Our captain exclaimed: 'Holey-moley!',
'A batsman was struggling on nought', 'A courteous spin-bowler called Bubblebrew', 'The reason I live my life my way', 'A rambler, much lighter than cork', 'A health-concious Rector named Jessop', 'An incompetent plumber from Goole', 'The spy who came in from the cold', 'I think our Quiz Team may be cursed', 'A traffic-cop based in the Bronx', 'A miser was driving his Rolls', 'Chocoholic, the great General Custer',
'A forgetful old fool called O'Reilly', 'An upper-crust wally named Willy', 'There's a chap who's quite happy to boast', 'A man who'd spent years on the roads', 'A little old granny called Maud', 'An Irish roadworker named Flynn', 'Asked the marvellous illusionist, Zorro:', 'As pets locusts aren't quite the ticket', 'An elderly bloodhound called Rix', 'Two grizzlies with not much to do', 'An old boxer dog named McDuff', 'A rodent, a bit of a rat', 'An overweight budgie named Billy', 'A starter, a main course, a sweet', 'An old alcoholic called Bill', 'I'll start with the mulligatawny', 'A greengrocer told me, quite stroppily', 'I work in a patisserie', 'I adore the Italian deli' and other limericks copyright © Charlotte McBee 2008.

DON NIXON
'A limerick writer from Bude', 'A haute cuisine author who sells', 'An orchestra caused quite a fuss', 'A devious gardener from Leeds' and 'It's clear Peter Rabbit's a rotter' copyright © Don Nixon 2008.

CATHERINE OSBORN
'There was an old fellow from Pinner' copyright © Catherine Osborn 2008.

ELEANOR ROGERS
'Van Gogh groaned: 'It's wrecked my career'', 'A missionary, I once heard tell', 'To be, or perhaps, not to be', 'Some chimpanzees sat in a Zoo', 'Michaelangelo moaned: 'My head's reeling'', 'Some mates once invited Will Shakespeare', 'Marco Polo, returned from Peking', 'In Loch Ness a monster once stayed', 'I would like to point out, Mr Lear' and 'King Canute sat alone on the beach' copyright © Eleanor Rogers 2008.

RON RUBIN
'Golf is a four-letter word', 'Ice Hockey is played at great speeds', 'Basketball, a most interesting sport', 'Now Baseball is truly the ticket' and 'US Football though played with elan' copyright © Ron Rubin 2008.

MARGARET SKIPWORTH
'Jack Russell out walking one night' copyright © Margaret Skipworth 2008.

JANET SMITH
'Mrs Malaprop nurtured an animus', 'In the coutry, the graceful Miss Muffet', 'There was a young man from Thibet', 'There was a young man from Dunoon', 'A greedy young woman from Stoke', 'An impotent man from Niagra', 'James Bond is an agent I've heard', 'A violin player from Delhi', 'The pet shop said *she* was a *he*!', 'R Crusoe said to D Defoe:', 'Modern limerick verse is imbued', 'I have heard that the great Mr Lear' and 'Of limericks Jekyll's oblivious' copyright © Janet Smith 2008.

JOE SPALDING
'An athletic young fellow called Mike' and 'There was a young lady called Mary' copyright © Joe Spalding 2008, and reproduced with the permission of Mrs J Spalding.

MIKE SPILLIGAN
'Grab your gun! Let's go hunting for fun!', 'Said a chef, who thinks each of his dishes,', 'There was an old woman named Doris', 'An Italian lady named Vera', 'There's a café on t'far side of 'eath', 'The striker, a newly-signed star', 'A batter, named Fatty McPhatter', 'A basketball player named Small' and 'I asked Santa Claus for some bed-socks' copyright © Mike Spilligan 2008.

NIGEL STRATTON-DAWES
'There was a young lady called Tess' and 'There was a young lady called Claire' copyright © Nigel Stratton-Dawes 2008.

MARIAN SWINGER
'A flighty young lady from Deal', 'Two dinosaurs strolling, arms linked' and 'An unfortunate schoolboy called Pete', 'A small group of schoolgirls from Grays', 'A robber named Brian McGrew', 'A big bouncing baby called Brett', 'A hamster called Septimus Claw', 'A naughty young schoolboy from Datchet', 'A gluttonous schoolboy called Nick', 'A young mountaineer from Stock' and 'A daring young gymnast called Fritz' copyright © Marian Swinger 2008.

NICK TOCZEK
'In truth, in his youth, Babe Ruth', 'If everyone else was much smaller', 'An ambitious young baseball player' and 'To you Yanks, I have just this to say:' copyright © Nick Toczek 2008.

TOM WAYTS
'There's an ointment that makes willies bigger', 'A young Spaniard who's hung like a horse', 'A bit of a wanker named Willy', 'A naturist rambler named Ron', 'Prince Charming was worried to bits', 'Ex-telephonist Gladys, I'm told', 'A talented painter called Duff', 'A young lady whose breasts were quite wee', 'A golfer who drives with some force', 'A gorilla that lives in the Zoo', 'A barrel of lard known as Lyn', 'A bat and a bat in a cave', 'I may look fairly old and sedate', 'There was a young girl from Penzance', 'A keen lassie who has to have cock', 'A Hollywood star named De Niro', 'A friend has an end to his member', 'A whore for a bit of a joke', 'A well-endowed chap with a cock', 'A geneticist living in Rheims', 'Mickey's is bigger than Dickie's', 'A young lass with a prize-winning bum', 'There's a grouchy old farmer near Neath', 'A small Bed & Breakfast in Crete' and 'A chap on a diet of fruit' copyright © Tom Wayts 2008.

COLIN WEST
'I once gave a thirsty giraffe' copyright © Colin West 2008.

DENNIS WALKER
'A wizard and witch were surprised', 'Old Bill used to

play ukelele', 'To the castle the raging hordes thundered', 'She partied dressed as an Azalea', 'A bearded bounder called Morse', 'I have an Alsatian called Rover', 'An adventurous maiden, Antonia', 'Britain hopes to be able quite soon', 'When Randy appeared on Big Brother' and 'Bert's younger sister, Anita' copyright © Dennis Walker 2008.
LES WILKIE
'My dainty young Siamese cat', 'I knew a provincial old actor', 'A batsman
was heard to rejoice', 'A limerick writer called Fred', 'I once knew a writer of prose',
'I took a short holiday flight', 'A musician who lived in Caracas', 'There once was a writer in clay', 'I met a young man from Korea', 'I've studied the stars big and bright',
'I knew a purveyor of pills', 'A player just turned twenty-one', 'A hungry stone-ager from Leeds', 'I've heard of a servant, quite civil' and 'A golfer, employing a wedge'
copyright © Les Wilkie 2008.

We are also grateful for permission to include the following previously published limericks:

FROM THE ARMADA BOOK OF LIMERICKS and THE SECOND ARMADA BOOK OF LIMERICKS
Limericks copyright © Mary Danby and individual authors, and reproduced with the permission of Mary Danby and individual authors.
ISAAC ASIMOV
'On the beach,' said John sadly, 'There's such', 'There was a young man of Belgrade' and 'There was a young lady of Ealing' copyright © Isaac Asimov, previously published in *Lecherous Limericks* by Isaac Asimov (Panther Books). All efforts to trace the copyright holder were unsuccessful.
GERARD BENSON
'There was a young girl of Kilkee' and 'There was a young princess, Snow White', previously published in *The Penguin Book of Limericks* compiled and edited by EO Parrott (Penguin Books) 1983; 'There once was a knight called Sir Bert', previously published in *Loopy Limericks* picked by John Foster (Collins) 2001; 'LIM (There once was a bard of Hong Kong)', previously published in *Evidence of Elephants* (Viking) 1995; and 'There was nothing, then dinosaurs, then', previously published in *Omba Balomba* by Gerard Benson (Smith/Doorstop) 2005, copyright Gerard Benson and reproduced with the permission of the author.
JOHN BETJEMAN
'Summer' copyright © The Estate of John Betjeman, previously published in
The Best of Betjeman (John Murray Ltd), and reproduced with the permission of
Aitken Alexander Associates.
CYRIL BIBBY
'A young electrician from Distance', 'A lock-keeper's lass in Upavon', 'The train that was due to depart', 'When cars are left here for repair', 'In the shed at the end of the mews', 'Dear Doctor, please look at young Millie', 'Dear Mom, I am lernin to spel' and 'Dear Prof, in reply to your note' copyright © Cyril

Bibby, previously published in *The Art of The Limerick* by Cyril Bibby (The Research Publishing Co) 1978. All efforts to trace the copyright holder were unsuccessful.
FROM THE BLUE PETER BOOK OF LIMERICKS
'A hungry old goat named Heather', 'There was a young man of Arbroath', 'There was a young laddie called Tony', 'There was a young lad called Davy', 'There was a young lady of Leeds', 'There is a maths teacher called Rundle', 'There was an old teacher named Brass', 'There was a young man with a horse', 'There was a young fellow from Crewe', 'There was a composer called Strauss', 'There was once a brown dog called Spot', 'A certain young goalie called Finn', 'There was a poor moggie from Hyde', 'There was a young girl called Pam', 'My brother's name is Keith', 'A certain young fellow called Peter', 'There was a young fellow called Fred' and 'There was a young cannibal Ned' copyright © the individual authors, previously published in *The Blue Peter Book of Limericks* Edited by Biddy Baxter & Rosemary Gill (Pan Books/BBC) 1972.
All efforts to trace the copyright holder/s were unsuccessful.
NM BODECKER
'There was an old crusty mechanic', 'A modest but talented duckling', 'An old school bus driver from Deering', 'An elderly hound of Cohasset', 'Some travellers lugging valises', 'This middle-aged person of Keene', 'This far-roaming lass from Milwaukee', 'A person of taste in Aruba', 'A splendiferous person of Haxey', 'A sheikh from the mountains of Riff', 'A tiresome person in Corning' and 'A little old person of Nigg' copyright © NM Bodecker, previously published in *The Penguin Book of Limericks* and
A Person from Britain whose Head was the Shape of a Mitten JM Bodecker (JM Dent
& Sons Ltd, a division of The Orion Publishing Group) 1980, and reproduced with permission. All efforts to trace the copyright holder were unsuccessful.
TONY CHANNON
'A man seeking moral direction' copyright © Tony Channon, previously published in
Rhymes for an Idle Moment (Eliton Books) 2002, and reproduced with the permission of the author.
PAUL COOKSON
'Big Lee Merick (A tower of strength in each game)' copyright © Paul Cookson 2008,
previously published in *Give Us a Goal* by Paul Cookson (Macmillan) 2004, and reproduced with the permission of the author.
GINA DOUTHWAITE
'Great Ginnel Grinner' copyright © Gina Douthwaite, previously published in
Young Hippo Spooky Poems (Scholastic), and reproduced with the permission of Andrew Mann Ltd.
GAVIN EWART
'The Semantic Limerick,' 'The Irish are great talkers' and 'Life is sad and so slow and so cold' copyright © Gavin Ewart, previously published in *The Collected Ewart* Gavin Ewart (Hutchinson) and *The Oxford Book of Comic Verse* edited by John Gross (OUP) 1995, and reproduced with the permission of Mrs Margo Ewart.
NOEL FORD

ACKNOWLEDGMENTS

'Please tell me,' the chimpanzee said', 'A polar bear grumbled: 'I wish', 'An ostrich, prim. proper and pert', 'A chicken named Little once said', 'In a frame of mind far from serene', 'I learned when attending night school', 'A young scout named Benjamin Potts', 'An elephant known as Selina', 'A flamingo I bought in a sale', 'A glow-worm once asked a close friend', 'Could you answer a small question, please?', 'Stinging nettles are painful to some', 'A promising artistic weasel', 'If you're out shooting birds just for fun', 'The stinkiest animal ever' and 'As my husky-team started to sneeze' copyright © Noel Ford, previously published in Limeroons by Noel Ford (Puffin) 1991, and reproduced with the permission of Penguin Group (UK).

PAM GIDNEY
'There was a young fellow named Tom' copyright © Pam Gidney, previously published in Loopy Limericks picked by John Foster (Collins) 2001, and reproduced with the permission of the author.

CATHERINE GRAHAM
'An affectionate barn owl flew', 'An incurable gambler named Fetter', 'When Henry the Eighth was a lad', 'A quick-witted sailor from Skye', 'A greedy young schoolboy named Mark', 'A professor of English called Shorter', 'Hypochondriacs, father and son', 'An animal lover named Cilla', 'A lazy young puppy named Jinx', 'One Saturday morning young Mike', 'One day a magician named Matt' and 'There was a magician from Stoke' copyright © Catherine Graham, previously published in The Armada Book of Limericks and The Second Armada Book of Limericks, and reproduced with the permission of the author.

FROM GREAT GREEN LIMERICKS
'When a neutron meets friendly uranium', 'Too long has this Earth of ours been', 'Said the Devil, with terrific mirth', 'There were two little green men from Mars', 'Is the beach still a nice place to play?', 'As aliens passed in their craft', 'The political colouring book', 'Oh, why does nobody mind?', 'One day when the petrol runs out', 'There was a young lady of Perth', 'The earth has been quite a success', 'In fifty years time I declare', 'An organic young gardener from Sale', 'A wildlife gardener named Reg', 'A man with a chemical spray', 'They are chopping the rainforest down', 'There was a young yuppie from Ware', 'Today we've achieved a finesse', 'There once lived a foolhardy race' and 'Said the seal to the salmon and otters' copyright © the individual authors, previously published in Great Green Limericks (A Star Book/WH Allen & Co) 1989. All efforts to trace the copyright holder/s were unsuccessful.

BILL GREENWELL
'The reason we're asked to endure', 'There was a young lady of Ulva', 'A glib little beer-buff from Troon', 'That rebellious rodent called Jerry', 'Shelley's death – was it really his wish', 'For his Campbell-Soup screen-prints, society's' and 'A hyena once bet he could laugh' copyright © Bill Greenwell, previously published in The Penguin Book of Limericks. All efforts to trace the copyright holder were unsuccessful.

WILLIS HALL
'He's rung his last bell!' mourners cried' and 'Cried Frankenstein's monster: 'By heck!' copyright © Willis Hall, previously published in Spooky Rhymes by Willis Hall (Hamlyn/Egmont), and reproduced with the permission of The Agency (London) Ltd.
All rights reserved and enquiries to The Agency (London) Ltd, 24 Pottery Lane, London W11 4LZ. info@theagency.co.uk

JOHN HEGLEY
'There once was an organic leek' and 'There once was a woman of Gwent' copyright © John Hegley, previously published in My Dog is a Carrot by John Hegley (Walker Books) and reproduced with the permission of PFD Agency.

MARY HOLTBY
'Said Mars when entangled with Venus:', copyright © Mary Holtby, previously published in The Penguin Book of Limericks, and reproduced with the permission of the author.

FROM I'M SORRY I HAVEN'T A CLUE
'There's a lady who reads Mills & Boon', 'The best way to read Conan Doyle', 'Having children,' said Evelyn Waugh', 'When drinking a cup of Earl Grey', 'When sipping a cup of Darjeeling', 'A radical curate from Brent', 'I once spent a weekend in Hove', 'I once spent a weekend in Brighton', 'When Santa gets bored in his grotto', 'There's something about oregano', 'A little-known fact about Plato', 'A Welshman who ate some Caerphilly', 'The odd thing about Cecil Rhodes', 'At an orgy old Julius Caesar', 'An exciting young poet named Keats', 'I once had a fully trained moth', 'I've a small breed of dog called a Scottie', 'A little-known fact about Liszt', 'While leafing my way through The Times', 'I saw in this morning's Express', 'There's a café in old Milton Keynes', 'Whenever I wear winklepickers' and 'Posing naked can often be fun' copyright © the individual authors, previously published in I'm Sorry I Haven't A Clue compiled by Jon Naismith (Orion Media) 1998. All efforts to trace the copyright holder/s were unsuccessful.

JOHN McKILLOP (J Michael Fitzjoseph)
'The actress said: 'Bishop, my dear', 'A butcher chirped: 'Madam. your mince', 'A lion was rumbling inside', 'Oh, Daddy, may I marry soon?', 'A soldier, just new in the reg', 'The weatherman stood by his map', 'How much is your haddock with crumbs?', 'The barber employed a new boy', 'A painter at Coldwater Zoo' and 'Oh, Mother, I can't be a nun' copyright © John McKillop, previously published in Limericks for Lunchbreaks (Seven Islands Press), and reproduced with the permission of the author.

COLIN McNAUGHTON
'Bully Boy McCoy' copyright © Colin McNaughton 1993, from Making Friends With Frankenstein by Colin McNaughton, and reproduced with the permission of Walker Books Ltd, London SE11 5HJ.
'The Oozily Woozily Plonk' copyright © Colin McNaughton 1999, from Wish You Were Here (And I Wasn't) by Colin McNaughton, and reproduced with permission of Walker Books Ltd, London SE11 5HJ.

OGDEN NASH
'A careless explorer called Blake', 'There was an old man in a trunk', 'There was an old man of Calcutta', 'There was a young lady called Harris', 'A cute secretary, none cuter' and 'A crusader's wife slipped from the garrison' copyright © Ogden Nash, previously published in *The Penguin Book of Limericks*, and reproduced with the permission of Curtis Brown Associates Ltd (New York), on behalf of the Estate of Ogden Nash.

MICHAEL PALIN
'A greedy young fellow called Wrench', 'There once was a fellow called God', 'A Frenchman called Didier Brume', 'A batsman from Sydney called Fairlie', 'There was a gravedigger from Barnes', 'A young mountaineer called Vic', 'There was a young fellow called Priestley', 'A lady from Louth with a lisp', 'A javelin thrower called Vicky', and 'A very light sleeper called Lowndes and other limericks' copyright © Michael Palin, previously published in *Limericks* by Michael Palin (Hutchinson) 1985, and reproduced with the permission of the author.

ERIC PARROTT
'There was a young outlaw named Hood', 'A carpenter living in Crewe' and 'A bashful young fellow of Brighton' copyright © Eric Parrott, previously published in *The Penguin Book of Limericks* compiled and edited by EO Parrott (Penguin Books) 1983, and reproduced with the permission of Mrs Tricia Parrott.

FROM THE PENGUIN BOOK OF LIMERICKS
'The limerick is furtive and mean', 'It needn't have ribaldry's taint', 'There was an old man of Bengal', 'There was a young man of Montrose', 'The ankle's chief end is exposiery', 'In New Orleans dwelt a young Creole', 'A candid professor confesses', 'Said a pupil of Einstein: 'It's rotten'', 'A psychiatrist fellow from Rye', 'Though your dreams may seem normal and right', 'Wee Jamie, a canny young Scot', 'Two earnest young fellows named Wright', 'King Richard, in one of his rages', 'It is clear that Napolean's Queen', 'Said Nelson at his most la-di-da-di', 'The trouble with General Sherman', 'There was an old cynic who said', 'As the natives got ready to serve', 'The Hoover, in grim silence, sat', 'A retired Civil Servant from Gateley', 'Princess,' said the frog, 'do not wince!', 'There was a young boy, Jack Horner', 'A platinum blonde, Goldilocks', 'Said Old father William: 'I'm humble'', 'There once was an artist called Pat', 'There was a young fellow named Sydney', 'It's a nightmare that horrifies hakes',
'I once took my girl to Southend', 'So obese is my cousin from Hendon', 'I once knew a spinster of Staines', 'Undressing a maiden called Sue', 'The Chief Stewardess of a Boeing', 'A naïve young lady of Cork', 'A millionaire filled with elation', 'Said a tripper:
'Oh, joy, to have found', 'If no pain were, how judge we of Pleasure?', 'The limerick issued from Lear', 'A fiery young fellow called Bryant', 'There was a young lady named Miller', 'I've combed out my beard and I've found', 'No Portugeses lady is nautical',
'A canner, exceedingly canny', 'A teacher of tots at Uttoxeter', 'A lass of curvaceous physique', 'There was a young lady of Lundy', 'There was a young

fellow called Shit', 'A cynic says: 'Now that we know'', 'Said a practical thinker: 'One should'', 'I suppose I could try if I chose', 'A wily old writer called Maugham', 'There once was a fellow called Hyde', 'Having rid Hamelin town of its vermin', 'There was a young chap so benighted', 'Sardines seem to get out of hand', 'An old gourmet who's grown somewhat stout', 'A young couple who lived at 'The Laurels', 'Most women get married it's true', 'Three Aldis, not one of them dim', 'A prostitute living in London' and 'A slow-footed stockman called Beales' copyright © the individual authors. All efforts to trace the copyright holder/s were unsuccessful.

CYRIL RAY
'At last I've seduced the au pair' and 'I was sitting there, taking my ease' copyright © Cyril Ray, previously published in *Lickerish Limericks* by Cyril Ray (JM Dent & Sons Ltd) and *The Penguin Book of Limericks*, and reproduced with the kind permission of Mrs Elizabeth Ray.

FRANK RICHARDS
'Said Wilbur Wright: 'Oh, this is grand'', 'Come now,' said Bell, 'this is choice',
'Said Wellington: 'What's the location'', 'The immaculate Sir Walter Raleigh', 'Said the vet as he looked at my pet', 'Victoria said: 'We've no quarrel'', 'In Pinter's new play that's now running', 'A monkey exclaimed with great glee', 'George Washington said to his dad', 'A boastful young fellow of Neath', 'George Stephenson said: 'These repairs'', 'Said a boastful young student from Hayes', 'A Victorian gent said: 'This dance'', 'Great-grandfather at Waterloo' and 'Rupert Murdoch, with glee, shouted: 'What', previously published in *The Penguin Book of Limericks*; and other limericks, previously published variously in *Limerick Delight* chosen by EO Parrott (Puffin Books) 1985, and *The Armada Book of Limericks*, copyright © Frank Richards and reproduced with the permission of the author.

RON RUBIN
'There was an old sultan of Saudi', 'A gentleman dining in Bude', 'Said a Yank, who was over from Yonkers', 'There was a young girl called Amanda', 'There was an old wizard of Rhodes', 'There was an old Man in the Moon', 'Now Len, you're an artistic lad', ''What,' said our teacher, Miss Pink', 'There was a stout lady of Dorset', 'Said the boa to his wife: 'Don't you find', 'Said Bert, who's a bit of a wally', 'When had up for pilfering, Percival', 'There was an old Abbot of Nice', 'An Astronomer Royal called Carruthers', 'As he finished his dainty first course', 'A naturalist of Beirut', 'There was a young poet called Sean', 'There was an old man of Bordeaux', 'Those beasts at the zoo,' said young Gus', 'There was an old man of Cambodia', 'There was a young sailor called Mort', 'Said a spoilt senorita of Ronda', 'A learned young lady called Betty', 'There was an old preacher called Herman', 'A lazy housewife from Spokane', 'A learned professor from Jackson', 'There was an old Aussie called Short', 'There was an old cowhand called Jess', copyright © Ron Rubin, previously published in *A Child's Garden of Limericks* by Ron Rubin & Mabyn Aita (Useful Music), and reproduced with the permission of the author.

Other limericks copyright © Ron Rubin, previously published variously in *Out on a Limerick* (New Millenium), *A Medley of Musical Limericks*, *The Penguin Book of Limericks*, *How to be Well-Versed in Poetry* (Viking/Penguin) 1998, *Rhythm 'n' Rhyme* (Arrival Press) 1996, *The New Statesman*, *The Spectator*, *Mayfair* and *Forum*, and reproduced with the permission of the author.

STANLEY J SHARPLESS
'There was a young lady...tut,tut!', 'Archimedes, the early truth-seeker', 'Marconi, whose ardour was tireless', 'Monsieur Gauguin? 'E's gone to Tahiti', 'Widow (conscious that time's on the wing)' and 'There was a young girl from Uttoxeter' copyright © Stanley J Sharpless, previously published in *The Penguin Book of Limericks*, and reproduced with the permission of Campbell Thomson & McLaughlin Ltd.

MARIAN SWINGER
'A jolly old fellow in red' and 'Mr Hullabaloo went to bed in a shoe', copyright © Marian Swinger, previously published in *Read Me Out Loud!* chosen by Nick Toczek & Paul Cookson (Macmillan Children's Books) 2007 and *Cockadoodle Moo* compiled by John Foster (OUP) 2001 respectively, and reproduced with the permission of the author.

NICK TOCZEK
'Advice for Spacemen' and 'The double-bass boom of the bittern' copyright © Nick Toczek, previously published in *Read Me Out Loud!* chosen by Nick Toczek & Paul Cookson (Macmillan Children's Books) 2007, and reproduced with the permission of the author.

COLIN WEST
'I'm a bit of a wasp with a worry', copyright © Colin West 2008, previously published in *The Best of West* (Hutchinson) 1990, and reproduced with the permission of the author.

ROGER WODDIS
'Think of those yummy fishfingers' and 'There was an old man with a beard' copyright © Roger Woddis, previously published in *The Kingfisher Book of Comic Verse* and *The Penguin Book of Limericks* respectively. All efforts to trace the copyright holder were unsuccessful.

ANTONY WOOTTEN
'A limerick tells of a scene', 'A boomerang maker named Wayne', 'A poet, the great Rimmer-Hicks', 'There once was a fellow from Gwent', 'A man who made hats in East-Filby', 'A ghost by the name of McGraw', 'A circus ring-master named Mike', 'An Antarctic penguin named Wayne', 'There once was a fellow named Price', 'An animal lover named Jack', 'Julie, a friend of a friend', 'Jack who had no airs and graces', 'There once was a fellow named Reece', 'A couple of fellows named Wright', 'St George spent the bulk of his life', 'An odd little fellow named Sam', 'There once was a fellow named Bysshe' and ' There is a young woman named Shirley' copyright © Antony Wootten, previously published in *There was an Old Fellow from Tring...* by Antony Wootten (Electric Monk Publishing) 2000. All efforts to trace the copyright holder were unsuccessful.

Every effort has been made to trace copyright holders. We would appreciate hearing from any copyright holders not acknowledged here.

Special thanks, for a variety of good reasons, are due to: Gerard Benson, Margaret Brace, Charlotte Bruton (Campbell Thomson & McLaughlin Ltd), Cirencester Lending Library, Mary Danby, Bob Dobson (Landy Publishing), Lisa Dowdeswell (The Society of Authors), Pete Duncan, Mrs Margo Ewart, Jonathan Eyers (Bloomsbury Publishing Plc), Sheila Hopkins, De'Anne Jean-Jacques (The Authors Licensing & Collecting Society Ltd), Reg Lynes, Liam Matthews, Charlotte McBee, John McKillop, Monmouth Lending Library, The National Library of Wales, Amy Pfahlert (The Society of Authors), Mrs Elizabeth Ray, FW Rees, Frank Richards, Ron Rubin, Inge & Gerd Schairer, Mike Spilligan, Stephanie Stahl (Macmillan's Children's Books), Nick Toczek, Tom Wayts, Colin West and Les Wilkie.

Index

Entries are selected from first lines only and comprise names of persons and places, key words and phrases.